Praise for Allan R. Bonilla's *I'm in the Principal's Seat, Now What? The Story of a Turnaround Principal*

I'm in the Principal's Seat, Now What? by Dr. Allan Bonilla is the kind of book that appears once in a decade. Bonilla became the principal of a large failing school in Dade County, Florida, succeeded in turning the school into an exemplary school, remained in that school for fourteen years, and tells his story through evidence-based examples of team building, school culture, principal visibility, and so much more. This book will appeal to any school administrator interested in leadership and practical options for helping a failing school become better, making a gifted school better, and anything in between. It is destined to become a landmark book.

Mark F. Goldberg, PhD, Education Writer and Book Editor
Austin, TX

In this immensely practical and powerful book, Dr. Allan Bonilla avoids the typical slogans about school culture and instead provides readers with the hard truths of leadership. Although Bonilla is a successful turnaround school leader, this book is valuable for leaders of high-performing schools as well as those in need of significant change. Moreover, both new and experienced leaders will benefit from the relentless emphasis on human connections in these pages. I particularly appreciate the author's iconoclastic approach to leadership visibility as he demonstrates that visibility in the lunchroom, hallways, and sidewalks is as important as visibility in the classroom. Looking through the eyes of the student, Bonilla appeals to leaders to make a human connection, preferring relationships over checklists and impact over appearances. Finally, this book provides an impressive mandate for the support of elective subjects, including arts and athletics, to save students from academic failure. Bonilla poignantly reminds us that electives are not a competitor for academic achievement, but a necessary support for them. The "Afterthoughts and Reflections" at the end of each chapter make this an ideal book for faculty book studies. I hope that it will generate vigorous discussions, constructive controversy, and as the author suggests, a few tears, all in the pursuit of a better understanding of helping our students.

Douglas Reeves, PhD
The Center for Successful Leadership
Denver, CO

This book is sure to be a must-have for every beginning and experienced principal. With Allan's experience as a successful principal in a struggling school, combined with his knowledge of leadership coaching, readers will gain inspiration and solid strategies to be equally successful.

Karla Reiss, Education Consultant
Certified Professional Coach and Corwin Author
President, The Change Place, LLC
Boulder, CO

As a veteran of twenty-one years in the principalship, I recommend this work to new and even seasoned principals who wish to continue to grow professionally. This is a thought-provoking work—one from which we can all learn.

David G. Daniels, High School Principal
Susquehanna Valley Senior High School
Conklin, NY

I'm in the Principal's Seat, Now What? provides a realistic, relevant view of how to be a principal in a changing environment. The power of the ideas and strategies is seen in the success of the school! This book is a must-read for those studying to be a principal or newly placed in a principalship.

Dr. Elizabeth J. Lolli, Superintendent
Monroe Local School District
Monroe, OH

I'm in the Principal's Seat, Now What? is a structured recipe for what matters most in school turnaround. The significant strategies are a visual road map for leading change and providing a quality education and high achievement for all students.

Suzanne Link Gimenez
Retired School Turnaround Principal
Devonshire Elementary
Charlotte-Mecklenburg School System
Charlotte, NC

It has been a privilege and pleasure over the past two years to listen to Allan as he shared with me his dream of writing a book that would assist in the transformation of low-performing schools. I quickly realized how much value this book would be to leaders of the many low-performing schools I was visiting as a turnaround consultant. I look forward to recommending this book to all my clients!

Mike Cave, MEd, School Turnaround Specialist
and Certified Educational Leadership Coach
Dripping Springs, TX

I'm in the Principal's Seat, Now What? is a practical yet powerful book that provides valuable insight into time-tested principles needed to turnaround any institution of learning. This back-to-basics book is designed to help school leaders create a culture of academic excellence.

Eric Acosta, EdS, Principal
Miami-Dade County Public Schools
Hialeah, FL

As a rookie administrator, I was placed under the supervision of Dr. Bonilla. I quickly learned that creating a positive culture, establishing a mission of academic success, and being visible are essential keys to being an effective school leader.

Dr. Bonilla uses simple and pragmatic approaches to organizational leadership that promotes universal buy-in from all stakeholders. His experience and on-the-job strategies should be a guide for all school and/or district administrators.

Manuel Ferrer, EdD
The Education Doctor, Inc.
Ft. Lauderdale, FL

In his book *I'm in the Principal's Seat, Now What?*, Dr. Allan Bonilla has done a masterful job of depicting responsibilities and duties that a school principal faces on a daily basis in the performance of his or her duties. I consider this book a must-read for every aspiring school principal who wishes to gain an insight into the role that he or she will play as a school principal.

Dr. Ada B. Hernandez, Retired Principal
Miami Dade County Public Schools System
Interns' Supervisor for Florida International University
Miami, FL

For ten years I've had the personal and professional gratification of closely and enthusiastically observing Dr. Allan Bonilla "walk the talk" and "be in the principal's seat" at Palm Springs Middle School in Miami. As his consultant on instruction, curriculum, and student learning, I found that his leadership engendered one of the most exciting and productive learning communities I've encountered as a consultant, teacher, leader, and professor. *I'm in the Principal's Seat, Now What?* is a "must" resource for every serious school leader!

Dr. Clint Bunke, National Leadership
Consultant and Reform Specialist
President, CDRM Corp.
Marco Island, FL

As a professor in the graduate school of education, I find that these strategies would be an excellent addition to teacher education courses, school operations, and management.

Dr. Steven Roth, Professor
Keiser University
Ft. Lauderdale, FL

"If you talk the talk, then you must walk the walk." Dr. Allan Bonilla is one prime example of an administrator who did just that in turning around a school that was at the lower rungs of a ladder and who elevated the staff and students through the prescription he set forth. The triad of relationships, collaboration, and team building are the key ingredients to changing a school's culture. Allan orchestrated and coordinated the faculty, the staff, and all of the stakeholders so the students could achieve their best. His plan was carried out daily by being visible throughout the day (morning, afternoons, evenings, and weekends) to parents, teachers, students, and community leaders, and I saw this as one of Dr. Bonilla's assistant principals. It is a prescription that will work at any school, any business, or any place where teamwork is the key to success. The principles Allan sets forth are the key ingredients for success in any setting where people working together can achieve anything if they work as a team. I, for one, am proud to have been a part of the success that Dr. Allan Bonilla achieved through his vision many years before this educational trend came into being.

> Howard Popowitz, Retired Administrator
> Miami-Dade County Public Schools
> American Book Services
> Pembroke Pines, FL

I'm in the Principal's Seat, Now What? is a must-read for all current and aspiring school site administrators. The book focuses on developing and implementing effective strategies that will transform schools from ordinary to exemplary learning institutions. The book was authored by Dr. Allan Bonilla, who distinguished himself serving as principal of one of the district's most challenging schools. Dr. Bonilla is recognized as an effective principal, having received the Principal of the Year distinction from the nation's fourth largest school district.

> Delio G. Diaz, Executive Director
> Dade Association of School Administrators (DASA)
> Miami, FL

Dr. Bonilla's book is a true and refreshing account and how-to guide. His extensive experience and knowledge result in a powerful combination that guarantees achievement and educational excellence.

> Martha Montiel, Administrative Director
> Education Transformation Office (ETO) at the
> Miami-Dade County Public Schools
> Miami, FL

The how-to guide, coupled with practical experience, adds authority to the author's voice. With essential questions at the end of the chapters, this work will provide a thoughtful and compelling read for new and veteran administrators alike.

> Rick Yee, Principal
> McAuliffe School
> Saratoga, CA

The theme of visibility presented has already challenged my thinking and provoked reflection on my current and previous practice. It has helped me to see gaps and holes that may have been there. This text would support my work with principals in helping them to see these as key traits/practices.

Arnna Graham, Leadership Coach
Vanderbilt University
Nashville, TN

I am taken by Allan's approach to learning and leadership. He recognizes that culture matters—a lot—and he offers specific strategies to help everyone in a school learn and grow.

Thomas R. Hoerr, Author and Columnist
Head of the New City School
St. Louis, MO

I'm in the Principal's Seat, Now What? provides a practical guide for building a school on the vision that each student matters. Given the right organizational structure and climate, teachers will take ownership of problems; will implement proven, practical solutions; and will grow from good to great when they are supported by their principals. Middle grades and high school principals serving in low-performing, challenging schools will gain great wisdom and insight for creating a high-touch, high-performance culture for students and teachers that will result in improved outcomes in attendance, performance, and student engagement. This book provides a vision for making parents a partner in the process, celebrating student and faculty growth experiences, and building healthy competition.

Dr. Gene Bottoms, SREB Senior Vice President
Founder and Director, High Schools That Work
Atlanta, GA

I'm in the Principal's Seat, Now What?

I'm in the Principal's Seat, Now What?

The Story of a Turnaround Principal

Allan R. Bonilla, EdD

CORWIN
A SAGE Company

CORWIN
A SAGE Company

FOR INFORMATION:

Corwin
A SAGE Company
2455 Teller Road
Thousand Oaks, California 91320
(800) 233-9936
www.corwin.com

SAGE Publications Ltd.
1 Oliver's Yard
55 City Road
London EC1Y 1SP
United Kingdom

SAGE Publications India Pvt. Ltd.
B 1/I 1 Mohan Cooperative Industrial Area
Mathura Road, New Delhi 110 044
India

SAGE Publications Asia-Pacific Pte. Ltd.
3 Church Street
#10-04 Samsung Hub
Singapore 049483

Printed in the United States of America

Library of Congress Cataloging-in-Publication Data

A catalog record of this book is available from the Library of Congress.

ISBN: 978-1-4522-7434-8

This book is printed on acid-free paper.

Acquisitions Editor: Arnis Burvikovs
Associate Editor: Desirée A. Bartlett
Editorial Assistants: Mayan White
                       and Ariel Price
Production Editor: Melanie Birdsall
Copy Editor: Jim Kelly
Typesetter: C&M Digitals (P) Ltd.
Proofreader: Victoria Reed-Castro
Indexer: Ellen Slavitz
Cover Designer: Michael Dubowe

13 14 15 16 17 10 9 8 7 6 5 4 3 2 1

Contents

Preface

Turnaround Success

It was my pleasure to have served as principal of a large urban middle school in the nation's fourth largest school district for some fourteen years. During those years, my faculty and I were able to transform a failing and unwanted school into one that was sought after, even by those from outside our attendance zone. The needs of at-risk students were met through a program that reduced the drop-out rate to a point at which it was recognized in a national Harvard University study. The daily attendance rate went from thirty-eighth to first in a district with fifty middle schools. Student achievement on standardized testing increased to the level of A as rated by the Florida Department of Education. Gifted student enrollment increased sufficiently to provide for a complete Gifted team at each grade level as well as a Gifted class for English language learners.

Leadership Focus

The contents of this book will assist a school leader in reaching success through the building of a positive school culture. Collaboration and team building and relationships form the foundation for what will bring about student achievement and teacher effectiveness. As I go about my current work as a conference speaker and leadership coach, I realize more and more that today's school leaders are being distracted from what is truly important in creating a great school. It was the German poet and philosopher Johann Wolfgang von Goethe who said, "Those things which matter most should never be at the mercy of those which matter least." In this book, I talk about what matters most: being a visible leader, delegating to promote collaboration, celebrating the successes of all, involving parents in a meaningful way, creating a positive culture, incorporating a coaching style, and much more.

Thoughts for All

Although this book could be considered a "how-to" volume for new principals and assistant principals, it is intended not only for this segment of education leaders. This is a book to be read and discussed by veteran principals, district educators, administrative teams, school board members, and, I hope, college students studying educational leadership and administration. The strategies presented are equally relevant for high schools, middle schools, and elementary schools, and for traditional as well as charter schools. *I'm in the Principal's Seat, Now What?* is based on evidential experience and supported by material from the world of business. Successful business practices can and should be emulated by school leaders.

Let's Create Exemplary Schools

Without a doubt, the ideas outlined in this book will help the reader create an exemplary school, which should be the goal of all principals. An exemplary school is one in which everyone is successful. Teachers are highly effective, motivated, and happy; students are meeting with success, whatever their levels; support staff are appreciated and contributing; and of course community involvement is evident. I was most fortunate to be recognized as Miami-Dade County's Principal of the Year for doing exactly what is discussed in this book. This award is presented annually, after a rigorous round of school-site visits and interviews, and goes to only 1 principal among the more than 300 K–12 principals in the district.

Each chapter focuses on a significant strategy: the power of visibility, delegating the smart way, success through collaboration, and more. Not only are actual examples and stories embedded within each chapter, but "hands-on" activities are provided at the conclusion of each chapter. Such things as a visibility checklist and a delegation chart and study questions will offer useful follow-up. In addition to business references from companies such as Google, Apple, and Facebook, there are links to useful references found on the Internet.

Why Is This Book Different, Unique, and Thought Provoking?

- It is written by an educator who spent forty years as a teacher, counselor, assistant principal, and principal, and it is based on real-life, evidence-based situations supported by leadership examples from the world of business. Understanding the leadership needed to create an exemplary school is key.
- It contains solutions to situations that are continually being faced by educators today, such as scheduling options, teacher retention, attendance improvement, at-risk student programs, facilitating change, promoting professional learning communities, parental involvement, teacher observation, and other challenges.
- The ideas presented can be immediately implemented by a leadership team at any given school regardless of its size or location or student population demographics. This is a true turnaround success story, accomplished without having to terminate faculty or close the school down.

Acknowledgments

There would be no story to tell were it not for the faculty members of Palm Springs Middle School, who so warmly welcomed me to their school at the start of this journey. They were eager for change and welcomed the opportunity to form what became a collaborative and caring family. To this day, some ten years after my departure, we are still connected and communicate regularly.

I was fortunate to work with three superior assistant principals as we began our journey. Booker Long was one of the most diplomatic individuals I ever had the pleasure of working with. Booker was a master at handling parental concerns. Howie Popowitz set us on the right curricular road and was my right hand in many ways. Melissa Wolin, our rookie assistant principal, took over the reins of our large exceptional education department and our program in English as a second language.

I may not have thought of writing a book on our turnaround success had I not met Arnis Burvikovs, executive editor at Corwin. It was Arnis who heard me speak at an ASCD convention and asked if I might be interested in preparing a book proposal. The years have passed since that meeting, and thoughts have become reality.

I owe a great deal of gratitude to Mark Goldberg, PhD, whom I met shortly after my arrival in Austin, Texas. Mark and I had much in common, as we were both principals and had New York backgrounds. However, he was the author of several successful books on school leadership, and I was not. Mark became my mentor and walked me through the process of submitting a book proposal and then getting started on the actual writing.

My coaching colleague, Mike Cave, a former principal in the Dripping Springs, Texas, school district, has been my coach for several years and has been with me since the start of my book-writing goal setting. I thank him for being my thinking partner.

I received a very pleasant and surprising invitation when the current Palm Springs Middle School principal, Eric Acosta, called and asked me to be present at a special school faculty meeting. Needless to say, it was very special to reunite with many of the staff who were present from the beginning and to meet the newer faculty members. It was during this visit, which included a tour of the school with classroom visits, that I realized I had another chapter to write, the final chapter, "Where We Are Now."

A tremendous expression of appreciation to my wife Pat, a teacher herself, who has always stood beside me and encouraged and supported all my endeavors and provided me with additional supporters in my two sons, Jeff and Scott, and their wives, Lisa and Trisha.

Last, what gives me hope for the future of education is watching the learning taking place through the eyes of my three grandchildren, Jack, Kate, and Myles.

Publisher's Acknowledgments

Corwin gratefully acknowledges the contributions of the following reviewers:

Scott Bailey
Assistant Professor
Stephen F. Austin State University
Nacogdoches, TX

David G. Daniels
High School Principal
Susquehanna Valley Senior High School
1040 Conklin Road
Conklin, NY

Arnna Graham
Leadership Coach and Curriculum Writer
Vanderbilt University
Abu Dhabi Education Council
Al Ain
United Arab Emirates

Elizabeth J. Lolli
Superintendent
Monroe Local School District
Monroe, OH

About the Author

Dr. Allan R. Bonilla was born in Orlando, Florida, a bit before Disney, and was raised in New York City, where he graduated from Forest Hills High School. After a brief stint at Hofstra College in New York, as well as a year and a half at California State Polytechnic University in Pomona, Allan returned to his home state of Florida, where he earned his BA from the University of Miami. Not knowing what career direction to take, he was told that Miami was in great need of teachers, and so there began a career in education that lasted forty years.

Teaching both English and Spanish at the middle and high school levels led this educator to a role as a counselor, after earning a master's degree at Barry University, and then to assistant principal positions in a half dozen middle schools. Feeling that he had the ideas and beliefs that could lead to creating successful schools, Allan pursued his doctorate in education at Nova University and was appointed principal of one of the largest and most troubled middle schools in the fourth largest school district in the nation.

Dr. Bonilla was indeed a "turnaround principal" and was recognized for his school's accomplishments by being selected Principal of the Year among a field of over 300 K–12 principals. Upon retiring from the Miami-Dade school system, Allan became a mentor to principals in the district and also a trainer with the Southern Regional Education Board.

Upon relocating to Austin, Texas, Allan became one of the first educators in the state to be trained through the Region X111 Education Service Center as a leadership coach. He has worked with some fifty educators, assisting them in working through difficult situations, achieving goals, and celebrating their accomplishments. In addition to coaching, Allan is a frequent speaker at state and national conferences, including those of ASCD, the National Association of

Elementary School Principals, the National Association of Secondary School Principals, High Schools That Work, National Charters, Texas Charters, and Florida Charters. He is also a faculty member of the National Principals Leadership Institute in New York City.

Allan's family includes his wife, two sons and their wives, and three genius grandchildren. Spare time, if any, is taken with reading to keep current with the changes and latest developments in the world of education.

Contact Allan at abonilla1@yahoo.com and www.coaching4 educators.com.

Building a Positive Culture

- It's People First, Then Programs
- Building the Foundation
- The Ripple Effect
- Creating the Climate

The foundation upon which to build a successful school has to be one of a positive school culture. Nothing can transform a poor school into an exemplary school without this foundation. Think for a moment of building your dream house. You have selected special windows to best control the interior climate. You have chosen attractive colors for the exterior as well as the interior. The appliances are all state of the art. You have even purchased all new furniture for this beautiful new home. The only problem: care was not taken with construction of the house, and it begins to crumble. The most important part of building a house, its basic structural integrity, was neglected in favor of the more visible enhancements.

The overriding emphasis in school improvement efforts, throughout the country, appears to be on programs rather than people. However, we are in a people business. We need to think of people first (teachers, students, parents) and then programs and evaluation, and accountability. State testing programs were to be the answer, along with the Common Core Curriculum, and professional development activities focusing on new initiatives. What is lacking is talk of making schools places where teachers can be respected and appreciated so that they can be at their best for students. Where are the conversations around creating schools where teachers can use their creativity and students can find joy in learning? The success my faculty and I had in turning around a failing school was indeed based on people first, then programs and initiatives, and professional development.

Culture Is the Common Core

So what is culture really about? You can find thousands of books written on the subject, not only for schools but for the business world as well. Corporate and organizational talk often centers on building culture. A web search on culture provides a limitless listing of resources, including articles, blog posts, books, and YouTube videos. At Palm Springs Middle School, in the Miami-Dade County Public Schools district, we felt that a culture built around respect, trust, and caring could provide the all-important foundation for our vision of an exemplary school. It was Jack Welch, the former CEO of General Electric and management guru, who said during a March 28, 2012, interview on CNBC, "Culture drives great results."

Culture building needs to come from leadership, from setting the example, and from being a positive role model. As an assistant principal, I worked at a school where the principal often resorted to shouting at teachers, even in the office area, where anyone could hear. He was not the role model one needs to create a solid foundation for success. I was an assistant principal at another school where all the early-arriving faculty members met in the cafeteria for coffee and conversation. The principal was always there enjoying the camaraderie. What a difference in role models! Be the model and set the example for what your vision of an exemplary school is. Albert Schweitzer, philosopher, theologian, and physician, said, "Example is not the main thing in influencing others. It is the only thing."

On September 13, 2012, the National Association of Elementary School Principals (NAESP) and the National Association of Secondary School Principals jointly released a report titled *Rethinking Principal Evaluation*. Building a positive culture was one of the six domains being considered. Indicators of performance in this domain include a principal's abilities to develop collaborative processes that affirm the school's mission, to ensure positive working conditions for teachers, to create time for instructional and teacher reflection, and to engage teachers in high-quality professional development. There should be no doubt that school culture must be a top priority for all principals.

The journal *School Administrator* published in August 2012 a "turnaround" article titled "Leading the Wagon Train" (Gimenez, 2012). This was the story of Suzanne Gimenez, who had been a successful principal for many years and was asked to produce the same successful results at a school that had been failing for several years. Among her many strategies was to introduce a family/team approach and create an environment of trust and honesty. Said Principal Gimenez, "We would work collaboratively to make it happen." To highlight her theme of togetherness, the school's theme song became "We Are Family" by Sister Sledge.

My very first faculty meeting was an especially important one because I was new to the school. I had been appointed approximately six weeks before the start of the school year, so I had an opportunity to meet some of the faculty members, and I also had an opportunity to hire a few new teachers to fill vacancies that had come about over the summer. For the most part, I was an unknown quantity, and although I had been an assistant principal for many years at several different schools, this was my first principalship. It was important for me to allow the faculty to see who I was, where I had been, what I had done, and what my vision for the school might be.

Do You Know My Name?

After my introduction, I explained to the faculty that we were going to view a short film that I hoped would clarify how we would look at students. The film was *Cipher in the Snow* (Whitaker & Atkinson, 1974), produced by Brigham Young University and now widely viewed on YouTube. It is the story of a young boy who dies unexpectedly, and his math teacher, who is asked to write the boy's obituary. Even though this teacher was the boy's favorite, the teacher hardly knew him. The boy was a cipher, an unknown number in the teacher's grade book. My question to the faculty: "Did we have students here who were overlooked as well?"

There were few dry eyes in the room by the end of the film, but it did send the message that we would truly be about caring for all students. We were going to begin to change our culture by looking at all students with a positive vision for their futures. There could be no more wholesale student failures and no more "writing off" students who appeared to be disinterested. Students would be valued and accepted in an environment where they could interact with caring people whom they could trust.

At a conference I attended many years ago, one of the presenters brought up the fact that many students go through their days without ever hearing their names called. If they are not part of a social circle and do not have many friends, they may never hear their names uttered by classmates. If teachers are not focused on names, or have forgotten how important one's name is to a person, a student has an even darker day. Many teachers issue orders such as "Pick up your paper" or "Move your seat," or they might say, "What is your question?" without using a student's name. What a difference it makes to a student when phrases such as the above are preceded by the student's name. We all know how good we feel when our names are remembered by others who are addressing us.

A practice we initiated, having teachers stand at their classroom doors to greet incoming students, greatly enhanced the personal relationships between teachers and students. Teachers could now acknowledge students with a nod or a smile at the very least and could even make personal comments. I had been at schools where students might enter a classroom to find the teacher seated at the desk, almost oblivious to the entering group. Although we hoped students would never be absent, it was comforting to a student who had been absent the day before to have a teacher say something like "We missed you yesterday."

I Care

Relationships between teachers and students set the stage for student learning. Without a positive relationship, there cannot be much growth. There is a statement I often think of when looking at teaching and learning: "I don't care what you know, until I know that you care." Students, just like teachers, want to know that they are cared about. The learning process is a very personal one, and young people need to feel good about what is happening in a classroom in order to produce maximum results. All of us who have been in education for any amount of time know that the best teachers are usually the ones who build caring relationships. We can all think back to our school days and recall a teacher or two who had a profound effect on us because they cared about us in a personal way. It was Dale Carnegie who said, "You can make more friends in two months by becoming interested in other people, than you can in two years by trying to get people interested in you."

Parade magazine, which is usually included in the Sunday editions of local newspapers, ran a wonderful and uplifting story titled "World's

Greatest Teacher" (Meltzer, 2012). It was the true account of a man returning to his junior high school in Miami, Florida, to visit a former teacher who was retiring. The man recounts how, as a ninth grader, he had just moved to Florida from New York and how most of his new teachers seemed to look past him. He felt that he was just one more student among hundreds. However, there was one teacher who took an interest in him and told him that he was good at something. That something she praised him on was his writing ability. She believed in him, and he believed what she said. Today, he is the successful author Brad Meltzer, writer of both fiction and nonfiction. Teachers do have powerful and long-lasting effects on all students.

Set the Tone

It is important for a school's leaders to teach by example. Teachers need to see their school administrators treating students with respect. If administrators go about their day shouting at students, the vibe will become contagious. Are the administrators friendly toward students, or do they ignore them when passing in the hallway? I believe that my practice of interacting with students in front of the school as they arrived each morning set an example of a positive adult-student relationship. Parents certainly appreciated seeing the principal mingling with their children on a daily basis, and this practice further emphasized to teachers what we were all about.

As will be discussed in Chapter 2, on visibility, the administrators and counselors spent time in the school cafeteria daily. Yes, we were monitoring behavior, but we were also building positive relationships with our students. One of our assistant principals, who enjoyed the game of chess, brought chessboards with him to the cafeteria and set up games for interested students. Most important, teachers knew of our cafeteria practice and observed the relationships for themselves when they came

> Setting positive examples is really the key.

to lunch. This was a true turnaround from the leadership practice that had existed previously. Setting positive examples is really the key.

We have all heard of the "ripple effect," probably as children when we threw a pebble in a pool of water and marveled at the ripples it made. Setting examples, and observing the ensuing results, can be compared with ripples in water. When teachers observed administrators actively engaging students in the hallways, they did the same. When teachers observed other adults greeting one another in a pleasant manner, they did the same. Students picked up on this as well. I recall vividly a student in the cafeteria saying to me, "You know why students like you? It's because you respect us." That was an important thing for me to hear, and it must have made an impression, because I still remember the incident so many years later.

Setting the tone for how things should be is extremely crucial. It cannot be done via memo, however. Setting the proper positive tone has to be an observable action. It is rather like the expression "to walk the talk." When parents, or any visitors for that matter, enter a school building, they should be greeted by individuals who are pleased to see them. Teachers need to see their administrators as positive, upbeat people. There is no room in an exemplary school for unhappy, complaining, moody individuals. Students also need to observe the adults in their schools as respectful and caring and positive people. As Robert J. Weintraub (2012), professor at Teachers College at Columbia University, said in a *Phi Delta Kappan* article, "forge strong partnerships with staff, parents and the broader community, lead by walking around, be happy, and create a family within the school."

How's the Climate?

It is interesting to note that more and more today, businesses are using surveys to determine if they are doing a good job in pleasing their customers. JetBlue Airways frequently sends out an online survey as a follow-up to a flight, and one of the questions is "Did the pilot come out of the cockpit to greet passengers before the flight?" Many doctors' offices are doing the same. Restaurants will even reward you if you go online and complete their surveys after your dining experience. Software designers are providing services to companies to assist in analyzing survey results.

Many, if not most, school districts do their own surveys as part of school improvement processes. Again, the purpose is to ascertain the "tone" of what a particular school is like. Does the school have a positive culture, for example? The Miami-Dade County Public Schools did an annual climate survey that surveyed parents, students, and faculty members at each one of the over 300 schools in the district. Questions centered on the "personal feelings" of the survey participants. Examples include "The school is a safe place," "The principal treats me with respect," "The administration is supportive of teachers," "My teachers always help me," and "My ideas are listened to." The rating scale ranged from "agree" to "disagree," with points in between.

Upon completion of each year's survey, the results were published in an annual compilation of all schools in the district as well as posted on the district's website.

The mission of the Baldrige Performance Excellence Program is to improve the competitiveness and performance of U.S. organizations. This prestigious program offers its own Education Criteria for Performance Excellence, which are used by many K–12 school districts around the country. The survey centers not only on what Baldrige calls "workforce satisfaction and engagement" but also on "customer satisfaction and engagement." Again, it is all about creating and focusing on a positive school climate.

Morale is most certainly a big factor in building a positive school culture. We often hear the word used with regard to organizations of any kind. If an organization's morale is high, people in the organization are happy with their situations. High morale indicates a positive culture. TheFreeDictionary.com defines "morale" as "the state of the spirits of a person or group as exhibited by confidence, cheerfulness, discipline, and willingness to perform assigned tasks," citing as a synonym "esprit de corps." We, as school leaders, want a school where morale is high and where everyone performs at high levels. We want our teachers to be as effective as they can possibly be so that our students can achieve at their very best. The most crucial function of a school leader is to create conditions where morale is always high, no matter what extenuating circumstances may exist.

> We want our teachers to be as effective as they can possibly be so that our students can achieve at their very best.

Be Happy

A major part of esprit de corps as mentioned in the above paragraph is cheerfulness. The *Collins English Dictionary* defines cheerfulness as "having a happy disposition; in good spirits." *Roget's Thesaurus* says that "happiness" and "cheerfulness" are synonyms. Positive culture building must include a focus on ensuring that our faculty members are happy people. Again, we are in a people business, and everything we hope to accomplish depends on the output of people. Happy teachers need to be a part of every classroom in our schools. Happiness is contagious, and happy teachers can lead to happy students with increased achievement levels.

Delivering Happiness, by Tony Hsieh (2010), reached number one on the *New York Times* bestseller list. Hsieh is the CEO of Zappos, the top online seller of shoes, which was acquired by Amazon for almost $1 billion. He talks about focusing on company culture as the number one priority and applying research from the science of happiness to running a business. The book's website (deliveringhappiness.com) states, "Tony shows how a very different kind of corporate culture is a powerful model for achieving success . . . by concentrating on the happiness of those around you, you can dramatically increase your own." This is a man who has proved what his philosophy can do. Let's do it too.

Dale Carnegie said, "Common sense is not common practice." It is common sense for administrators to greet teachers with a smile and a "good morning" whenever possible. It is common sense to look for positive comments to make to teachers and students. These and other little things make for happy teachers and happy students. Our faculty meetings always included coffee, tea, and cookies. Teachers were always provided with "goody bags" of desk supplies at the start of each school year. We did our best to see that all classrooms were in good repair and that new furnishings were provided whenever possible. Even small things can make people happy. Teachers were thrilled when they returned from summer break and found their classrooms filled with new student desks. We made sure that teachers had a comfortable place to eat their lunch or to have coffee in the mornings. One of the special things we did was to provide what we called a "faculty study," which was a room set aside for teachers to work on lesson plans or read professional journals or access computers during their planning periods.

Teachers knew that the administration truly cared about their well-being and their happiness. Schools, and the school environment, are often not the most accommodating entities. Limited budgets often prevent administrators from doing some of the more exceptional things they may want to do for teachers and students. However, a beautiful house does not make a successful home. The way we treat people says much more about who we are and what we are about.

Tal Ben-Shahar, PhD, was a successful Harvard professor who taught one of the most popular classes at that esteemed university. His classes on positive psychology, which combines scientific research with common sense, attract some 1,400 students per semester. The book he wrote, based on his Harvard lectures, is titled simply *Happier* (Ben-Shahar, 2007) and was a *New York Times* bestseller. Martin Seligman, the father of positive psychology, called the book "the backbone of the most popular course at Harvard." In Chapter 7, "Happiness in the Workplace," Ben-Shahar talked about creating conditions conducive to happiness.

It is the responsibility of a school leader to ensure, whenever possible, that teachers are happy in their work so that they can do their best for students. A book by Neila Connors (2000) with a most clever title, *If You Don't Feed the Teachers They Eat the Students!* is a wonderful reminder to all administrators of the importance of putting teachers' needs at the center of everything we do. In Chapter 2, "The Need to Feed," Neila wrote, "Administrators who make it a priority to treat teachers with respect, recognize invaluable contributions, and realize teachers are their best allies, see great things happen." In Chapter 3, "Creating the Ambiance," Neila used a quotation from Charles E. Bryan: "The quality of employees will be directly proportional to the quality of life you maintain for them."

> It is the responsibility of a school leader to ensure, whenever possible, that teachers are happy in their work so that they can do their best for students.

Principal magazine, the journal of the NAESP, published an article in its March/April 2008 issue on school culture by Steve Gruenert (2008), professor of educational administration, who wrote, "It seems that a happy teacher is considered a better teacher, and this attitude influences the quality of instruction." Gruenert went on, "If happy people truly perform better, then leaders must create conditions in which happiness thrives." We hear the term "effective teachers" used frequently when talking about what is needed in every classroom. It appears that the key to effective teaching may be found in the happiness level of the faculty members.

> It appears that the key to effective teaching may be found in the happiness level of the faculty members.

A wellness coach at About.com, Elizabeth Scott, said in a January 7, 2011, *Inc.* article, "The CEO's demeanor can directly affect the staff.... So, smile more often, talk about fun things ... or crack a joke" (Hames, 2011). I do believe that a principal needs to set the tone and walk the talk. There is no way for faculty members, or students for that matter, to be happy participants in daily school life if the principal is frequently seen as an unhappy person. We have all come across school leaders who may be unhappy in their personal lives and tend to bring their issues with them to school. We have all seen principals who are so concerned with administrative challenges that they are too preoccupied to show any form of positive emotion to their faculty. There can be no successful schools, regardless of the superb curricula they may have, or the state-of-the-art technology at their disposal, if there is unhappy leadership leading to unhappy teachers and unhappy students. As Craig Jelinek, the CEO of Costco, said, "Culture is not the most important thing, it is the only thing."

Afterthoughts and Reflections

What do I do to focus on teachers?

_____

_____

_____

What do I do to show I care about my students?

_____

_____

_____

How am I showing my interest in our parents?

_____

_____

_____

How do I/we recognize and celebrate our teachers, students, and parents?

_____

_____

_____

In what areas am I a role model for faculty and students?

_____

_____

_____

In what ways are we receiving feedback from parents, students, and faculty?

_____

_____

_____

How are we making our school a happy place?

_____

_____

_____

How do we set the tone and walk the talk?

_____

_____

_____

Check out climate surveys at

http://drs.dadeschools.net/SchoolClimateSurvey/SCS.asp

http://www.nist.gov/baldrige/publications/education_criteria.cfm

Structured Visibility

- Out and About
- See and Be Seen
- Observations Are Key
- Don't Forget the Students

As a school leader for some thirty years, counting my years as an assistant principal and a principal, I have come to realize that nothing is more important than the visibility of the leader. This holds true for elementary, middle, and high school. I have chosen to title this chapter "Structured Visibility" because of my belief that being a visible leader is not accomplished by chance, but is achieved through planning and purpose. A quick dictionary search will define "visibility" as "the state of being able to see or be seen," and this simple definition can provide the basis for our understanding of "structured visibility."

At the end of this chapter, there is a "visibility checklist" to which readers can refer. You may wish to look at it now and then read the chapter.

I think we all would agree that sitting in the principal's or assistant principal's office, for extended periods of time, provides little opportunity to actually see the goings-on of daily school life, or to be seen by those to whom we are leaders. Unfortunately, in today's school world, we are bombarded by e-mails, text messages, cell phone calls, and myriad other distractions, which tend to divert our focus from where it should be. The German writer and philosopher Johann

Wolfgang von Goethe (1749–1832) said, "Those things which matter most should never be at the mercy of those which matter least." What a wonderful quotation this is to remember as we go about our work creating exemplary schools, and begin to focus on "structured visibility."

> "Those things which matter most should never be at the mercy of those which matter least."
>
> —Johann Wolfgang von Goethe (1749–1832)

My definition of "structured visibility" is one that would focus on what is to be observed on a regular basis, how that might be accomplished, and who might be involved. For example, let's start with the morning arrival of students. Whom do parents see as they bring their children to school? If buses are involved, whom do the bus drivers see? If students walk to school or ride bikes, who is supervising this activity?

Early Morning

In my fourteen years as principal of a large middle school, there was obviously much early-morning activity. It was my habit to be in front of the school at least thirty minutes before the start of school. There I had the opportunity to observe student behavior and to be seen, not only by the students but also by parents dropping off their children. Bus drivers were always pleased to see the school's administrators in a supervisory role as well. I was assigned to the school to turn it around and was fortunate enough to be able to hire two assistant principals, in addition to the one who remained. My assistant principals often joined me around the perimeter of the school, unless they were involved in early-morning parent conferences.

The benefits of this early-morning visibility can be far reaching. Parents sometimes parked and walked over to me to ask questions. They always appreciated that I was outside to greet students. There is also an opportunity for a brief conversation or for a question with any staff member. Students also can become comfortable with their administrators by seeing them in an informal atmosphere before school actually begins. Much can be learned by an administrator while observing unstructured student behavior. What types of groups are forming? Who are the ringleaders? Which students might be loners? Is any type of bullying occurring?

As the new principal of a school that was regarded as "difficult," it was especially important for me to be visible. My early-morning visibility paid off greatly when I was able to turn around a potential gang-related problem. It was obvious to me, after a week or two of observation, that students had a pattern of congregating in the same general area as they awaited the start of school. One particular group, which I realized was the most challenging, always congregated at the southeast corner of the school campus. These students were our older population, most having failed at least one grade, and were not particularly interested in the academic side of school life. I made it my practice to stand near them on most mornings and to establish some sort of rapport.

One particular morning, I approached the group of perhaps fifteen students and invited them to meet with me in the school cafeteria after the day's morning announcements. They had no idea what this meeting would be about, but a meeting with the principal had to mean something big. Sure enough, they all arrived at the cafeteria with puzzled expressions. I shocked them with an invitation to see a play at a local theater. None of them had ever seen live theater, and few had ventured out of their immediate neighborhoods. This particular play, *Matador*, was the story of a young Mexican boy who dreamed of becoming a famous bullfighter. I knew this story would appeal to them, and to make it even better, the story was told through energetic modern rock music performed by a live band.

I must admit that when word got out to the teachers that the principal would be taking this particular group of students on a field trip to a theater, the feeling was that I was not of sane mind. These students had rarely received any positive reactions from faculty, nor had they ever been included in any extracurricular activity. On the other hand, as word got out to students, others asked to attend too. A bus was packed with almost fifty excited students, off to experience something new in their lives. The trip was a true success, and the play was enjoyed by all. Most important, we had formed a relationship. These students, who could have caused disruptions throughout the year, were now willing to become cooperative members of the student body. There is an often used phrase: "I don't care what you know, until I know that you care." These students knew that I cared about them and that maybe they did have a chance at a positive school life. Visibility is powerful! When we make the time to see and to use what we see, good things can happen.

> When we make the time to see and to use what we see, good things can happen.

End of Day

Visibility is also about prevention. Seeing and being seen can go a long way in preventing accidents and disruption. As important as visibility is in the morning, dismissal is also important, and more will be said about that later in the chapter. All schools are different, and the type of supervision will naturally vary depending on the size of the school, the number of students, and of course the ages of the students. A small elementary school with 300 students will require a different visibility plan than a high school with 3,000 students.

In a 2008 *Teacher* magazine article, members of the Teacher Leaders Network offered advice to a newly appointed principal in the rural Southeast. They said, "Be visible and accessible. It means a lot to teachers and other staff to see their principal in the corridors, in the cafeteria, and at after-school functions. Also, an open door policy makes the staff and parents comfortable with bringing issues directly to you rather than starting a whispering campaign."

A dismissal plan has to be concerned with the safety of students as they make their way home. Are there potentially hazardous street crossings? Is bike safety an issue? Is there a parent pickup area? Are buses parked safely? Which school personnel are assigned to which crucial areas? Is there a student parking lot? How about faculty members exiting in their cars? In addition to what becomes a routine procedure, visibility can go a long way in preventing incidents of a disruptive nature. At times, outsiders may come onto the school campus with intentions of causing problems. Our own students may decide to become involved in disruptive activities. Seeing and being seen are key to preventing what we don't want to happen on our campus. Prevention through "structured visibility" is a much better route to follow than attempting to resolve an issue later on.

Lunchtime

Another major area of student activity is the school cafeteria or lunchroom. Again, any time groups of students are congregating, supervision needs to be present. If I didn't already realize this simple fact of school supervision, it hit me hard when I learned that cafeteria food fights were routine events at my new school. Structured visibility had evidently not been in place, and cleaning up afterward took the place of prevention. One cannot have an orderly learning environment when unruly behavior is allowed to exist, especially in a large middle school where many students have been labeled difficult or disruptive. All schools are different and will have their unique issues to deal with. Not all will have food fights to contend with, but I have been in small elementary schools where cafeteria behavior left much to desire.

Although cafeteria supervision, or lunch duty, may not be a favorite time of day for many school administrators, it proved to be a most rewarding time for me and my fellow administrators. Of course, because of the type of behavior we encountered at our new school, we had to come up with a plan to turn around a completely unacceptable behavior pattern. The plan was a simple one: we would all be in the cafeteria every day, on our feet and walking around. As our definition of visibility states, "See and be seen." We monitored the behavior of our students carefully and were alert to any pending problems. Sometimes we even joined a table and ate with the students. Most significantly, students soon realized that all or most of the administrators would be there every day, in addition to the security monitors assigned to the cafeteria. The administrators engaged the students in conversation and could answer questions that were on the students' minds.

The negative aspects of cafeteria supervision turned around to reward us as students became comfortable with our presence and looked forward to interacting with us. We, especially being new to the school, quickly learned about our students in an informal way. Students knew they could ask questions of us and that we would give them honest answers. We got to know the formal and informal groups that all students form. Who sits together at certain tables? Which students always seem to be alone? Who are the ringleaders? One of our assistant principals found a group of students who were interested in chess and set up a table for them to play chess after their lunch.

An added part of our supervision plan came via the addition of our counseling staff. The counselors were asked to assist us, but were not required to do so. The reason for asking them was twofold: first, the students saw the counselors in a new light, and second, the counselors were able to spot students they wanted to see or help.

Because the cafeteria was usually quite crowded, and students entered on a continual basis, it was necessary to have adults stationed at the entrance to the three serving lines, usually the counselors. Again, the positive outcome of our counselors' involvement was that students had an opportunity to ask questions of their counselors. In many ways, this turned out to be a time saver and an efficient way to handle some issues for the counselors.

Another positive that came out of cafeteria supervision was that faculty members knew where they could find their administrators at lunchtime. When teachers had questions that needed quick answers, they could always be handled at lunchtime. In previous years, teachers never wanted to enter the school's cafeteria. Now they too were comfortable, and they appreciated the fact that the school's atmosphere was one of order and respect.

During my first year as principal, I came across a book titled *School Management by Wandering Around*, by Larry Frase and Robert Hertzel (2003). The title clearly spells out the authors' philosophy, and they could not have expressed it more clearly than by saying that an effective leader is "off his seat and on his feet." Although I knew I wanted to be, and certainly needed to be, a highly visible school leader, this book served to reinforce my belief. Education Secretary Arne Duncan said in a January 2010 *US News & World Report* interview, "In Race to the Top, what we talk about is great adults: great teachers and great principals. . . . There are no high-performing schools without great principals" (Clark, 2010). The article is recent, and my time as a principal started many years ago; nevertheless, I wanted to be that great principal.

Classroom Walk-Throughs

There was only one way I could accurately determine the strengths and weaknesses of my teachers, as well as the validity of our curriculum, and that was to do frequent classroom walk-throughs. The teachers were told at the beginning of the year that this would occur, that it would help me know them better and would be one more way I and my assistant principals would be visible. I made classroom visits a priority, setting aside at least one hour per day for this crucial activity.

Remember that we are talking about "structured visibility" and about putting the important things first as we go about being leaders. It is very easy to allow ourselves to be office bound and mostly invisible to parents, staff, and students. There are times when you need to be in your office, but you must make visibility a priority.

The benefits of classroom walk-throughs are far reaching. Most significantly, the principal or assistant principal will be able to see exactly what the teacher does on a regular basis. Walk-throughs are not formal observations, nor are they scheduled visits. They do give the supervising administrator the opportunity to see the type of learning that is going on in each classroom. For example, Is the teacher up and about or seated at the desk? Is the teacher working with groups of students? Is the teacher working one on one, providing assistance to an individual student? Is the teacher the "guide on the side" or the "sage on the stage"? Are students working cooperatively? Do students seem to know what the task at hand requires of them? Are all students involved and on task? What does the classroom look like? Is student work displayed? Are student resources available? How about technology? Are computers, laptops, tablets, SMART Boards, and printers in use?

There is no end to what will be observed during classroom walk-throughs, and not all things mentioned above may be seen on each visit. By making walk-throughs a priority in a structured visibility plan, the frequency of these visits will allow the observer to view significant aspects of teaching and learning over the period of repeated visits.

Both administrators and teachers understand that you will see good days, bad days, and everything in between. Keep in mind that walk-throughs should generally be brief and last no more than five minutes. The frequency of the visits provides the power to make a judgment about what is really happening. This process is many times more accurate than the once-a-year formal classroom observation, which has been part of administrator-teacher relationships in the past.

One might ask what happens after a classroom visit. Is there any type of feedback? Are notes taken? Are conferences held? A quick search on Amazon will yield dozens, if not hundreds, of resources on walk-throughs, from books to templates to guides. The idea, though, is not to make this most powerful part of an administrator's day a totally consuming project. Strength lies in simplicity. I have found that what is gleaned from walk-throughs can be used in interactions with teachers and students throughout the week. For instance, seeing a student in the cafeteria and commenting to her about the math work you observed is a positive way to build a relationship, as well as to reinforce the student's appreciation of learning. Commenting to a student you see after school about the great oral report she was presenting to her social studies class is another example of the positive use of classroom walk-throughs.

Teachers, like all of us, enjoy hearing positive feedback on how they are performing in their jobs. The walk-through process gives an administrator a perfect tool by which to reinforce for a teacher those positive observations enjoyed during a recent visit. As an example, administrators frequently see teachers as they leave at the end of the day. What a wonderful send-off for a teacher when the principal can comment on a great lesson he observed: "Wow, your students really loved their science activity today. Everyone was completely involved." Or "I was so pleased to see Johnny participating in his group. You have made great strides with him." The opportunities for positive interactions with teachers that walk-throughs can offer are endless.

Other forms of informal feedback, besides direct communication, might include a short note written by an administrator and placed in a teacher's mailbox: "Great lesson I walked into this morning"; "I love the way you tell stories to your class"; "It's great to see all students involved in your classroom activities." It only takes a few minutes out of an administrator's busy day to write a few notes, but the power is great. A teacher was quoted in a June 2008 issue of *Teacher* magazine as saying, "The nice note in my box on a random Thursday meant more than the time I won the 'Gold Star Award' because it was 'my turn.'" Teachers know that they will not always hear from me about a walk-through, but they will often get a note, or I'll run into them and say something.

Classroom walk-throughs also provide an excellent way to offer assistance to a teacher who may be experiencing difficulty with classroom management. It takes only a few visits for an administrator to ascertain which teachers may be in need of support in this crucial area. Teachers who have difficulty controlling student behavior know that this is a weakness for them and would certainly appreciate intervention in this area. Feedback to a teacher in this situation might include an offer of a professional development activity focused on classroom management. Another intervention might be an opportunity for the teacher to observe a master teacher in the same area of instruction. Of course, if the principal observes a particularly disruptive student in this teacher's class, it may be time for a student referral to a counselor or another member of the school's support staff.

Walk-throughs also provide a wonderful opportunity for the observer to determine the quality of the curriculum being taught. A teacher who may not be covering required material may be in need of support from the department chair. Perhaps a teacher is in need of resources to properly present new material. In some cases, the teacher's instructional methods may lack variety. Classroom visits allow an administrator to provide support wherever it is needed, and of course to realize where assistance is indeed necessary. Walk-throughs need not be conducted only by a school's administrators, but may also be conducted by department heads, counselors (to observe difficult students), and any subject-area coaches, a position that is now catching on in schools around the country.

On the Move

There is no "one size fits all" plan for visibility and supervision when groups of students are on the move. A small elementary school may have a plan whereby students are escorted by teachers as they move from classroom to lunchroom or from classroom to music or art room. A charter school of 150 students in one building may require teachers to be stationed at their classroom doors. The point is that students need supervision, and adults must be visible. The safety and security of all are the job of a campus leader.

My particular school had an enrollment of 1,800 middle school students, housed in several buildings; at one time, there were sixteen portable classrooms. A structured visibility plan meant that all adults had to be a part of supervision when students were moving from one classroom to another. Change of classes occurred six times each day, not counting arrival and dismissal. Preventing unpleasant happenings is a much wiser route to take than is remediating an issue after the fact. In a November 2006 article in *Principal Leadership*, retired middle school principal Robert Ruder wrote, "A principal's visibility assures students that there is someone in charge, someone to whom they can go to if they are experiencing difficulty, someone they can trust."

Our visibility plan was one that included all administrators, all counselors, all teachers, and security monitors. Administrators were assigned to different hallways along with counselors. In other words, everyone had his or her "post," with the principal free to monitor all areas. Teachers were required to be at their doorways to greet arriving students, as well as to be visible to students passing to other classes. This important part of school supervision produced many positive results. First, students soon became aware of the fact that they were under the eyes of adults at all times. Students who might have thought of causing a problem thought twice, realizing that they were probably being watched. This "change of class" plan was similar to our cafeteria plan, in that it provided needed supervision but produced positive benefits. Teachers and administrators also gave students a warm hello or asked how they had done on a test.

Many other positive benefits come out of a hall-monitoring plan. First of all, teachers standing at their doorways to greet students as they enter have a welcoming effect on students. A smile or nod from a teacher, or even a "Good morning, Maria," is a wonderful way for a student to start class. I have been in schools where teachers are seated at their desks, looking down at something, or even eating lunch or drinking coffee. The environment in such a

> The power of visibility has far-reaching positive effects and should not take second place to tasks that could be accomplished at noncrucial times.

classroom is totally different from that created by a welcoming teacher.

Second, administrators and counselors have an excellent opportunity to observe students' behavior as they move through the hallways. Which students always seem to be looking for trouble? Which students always seem to be running late? Are there incidents of bullying? Additionally, administrators and counselors have opportunities for brief interactions with students and for possible follow-up sessions later. Teachers, too, have an opportunity to ask questions or make comments. The power of visibility has far-reaching positive effects and should not take second place to tasks that could be accomplished at noncrucial times.

Lifelong Learners

Professional development activities provide another important opportunity for administrator visibility. Many schools have incorporated some form of professional learning communities, often referred to as PLCs. These groups may meet weekly or biweekly and may comprise grade-level or subject-area teachers. The meetings are conducted by the teachers themselves and serve as support and enrichment for participants. It is important to note that although this is a teacher-led activity, the involvement of administrators should not be overlooked. The principal and assistant principals should be aware of the meeting schedules of the various PLCs, and they should make it a habit to visit these meetings from time to time. The purpose of the visits should be to show that administrators are interested in what the PLCs are doing, not as a monitoring activity but as a way of showing interest, awareness, and support. Teachers do want to know that their principal is aware of and interested in what they are doing.

In a July 11, 2009, *New York Times* interview, Adam Bryant spoke with David C. Novak, the CEO of Yum Brands, which owns Pizza Hut and Taco Bell, among other well-known chain restaurants. Bryant asked, "What feedback do you get from your employees about your leadership?" Novak responded, "I continually get feedback about being even more visible. People want to see more and more of you. Even though I'm out in the marketplace all the time, you can't underestimate how important it is to be visible. When you're the leader, people want to see you. They want to touch you. They want to know that you are in tune with them."

In my particular middle school, we had several different groups meeting at regular times. One of the most structured groups was the middle school team, which met three mornings a week for thirty minutes before the start of the student day. Their purpose was two-fold: to confer with parents and to discuss team issues among themselves. Our counselors usually were part of these meetings, and the assistant principals attended when needed. It was my habit to look in on these team meetings, of which there were six, before I made my way to the front of the school for student arrival. My visibility at these meetings showed teachers that I considered them important and that I was interested in being a part of what they were doing. Two positive aspects of what might be called "meeting walk-throughs" was that I got to see parents who were participating in team conferences, and parents could appreciate the visibility of the principal.

Departments met biweekly and alternated with our School-Based Management/Shared Decision Making committees. These groups also met before school and were part of my visits as well. Our twice monthly faculty meetings rounded out our meeting schedule. These faculty meetings were usually devoted to some type of professional development activity and might be conducted by myself or an assistant principal or a department head. The point to be made is that the visibility of the school administration was always apparent.

Extra Curricula

After-school activities provide another opportunity for school leadership visibility. High schools, for instance, have a seemingly never ending round of activities, ranging from after-school club meetings to nighttime football games. Obviously, it is not possible for all administrators to be present at all events, but a plan of structured visibility will allow coverage to be provided where and when it is needed. Students and teachers realize that supervision for certain events is a necessity in order to provide for the security and safety of all involved. However, the second part of administrator visibility is the support provided to students and teachers, just by the presence of the school's leaders. Additionally, the opportunities for positive communication following an event are far reaching. Students love to hear a "Good job" from their principal, and teacher-sponsors appreciate a "Well done" from an administrator who was in attendance.

I was at one time an assistant principal at a magnet middle school for the visual and performing arts. This was a school that attracted students from a wide attendance area, and students had to audition in order to be accepted into the program. The students and their parents were very serious about their particular talents and looked for support and involvement from the school's administration. Nightly drama presentations, dance performances, and art shows were a large part of school life. My attendance at some of these events was always followed by a visit to the particular classroom the next day. I wanted the teacher, as well as the students, to know how much I appreciated their work and enjoyed their presentations. Again, visibility goes a long way in fostering positive relationships. Rather than being a chore, it is an opportunity that leads to greater communication and the creation of a supportive school culture.

Seen and Heard

One of my first major expenditures as a new principal was the purchase of televisions for all classrooms, along with the creation of a TV studio. Once the installations were complete, we were able to do our morning announcements via closed-circuit television, rather than via the public address system, with no visibility. It was my habit to be on the morning program daily, and after being introduced by our student anchors, I would say a few words about a good happening from the day before. These remarks might be about an excellent student attendance day or about a competition in which a student group participated. In a *BloombergBusinessweek* article from September 14, 2007, Jack and Suzy Welch wrote, "When an individual or a team does something notable, make a big deal of it. Announce it publically, talk about it at every opportunity. Hand out awards." In this simple way, positive remarks started the day, and teachers and students knew that the principal was indeed present.

> It is interesting to note that almost all school leaders value their visibility, yet only those who make being out and about a true priority actually succeed.

In an *Education World* survey of forty-three principals done in 2008, being visible, getting out of the office, and being seen all over the school were the most frequently identified qualities of a strong school leader (Hopkins, 2008). All but two of the forty-three principals surveyed included these qualities on their top-ten lists. It is interesting to note that almost all school leaders value their visibility, yet only those who make being out and about a true priority actually succeed. Following a plan of structured visibility, knowing where visibility will take you daily, and blocking distractions can be the most significant skills a leader will acquire.

Afterthoughts and Reflections

Typical Day on Campus

Hours spent in office _____

Hours spent in classroom walk-throughs _____

Hours spent "wandering around" _____

How satisfied am I, on a scale of 1 to 10, with the above results?

_____

Which of the above is most important to me?

_____

_____

_____

What changes can I make?

_____

_____

_____

Are there problem areas that might be improved upon through increased visibility by the principal, assistant principals, counselors, or other faculty members?

_____

_____

_____

What is our classroom walk-through plan? Do all administrators do walk-throughs? Are there other faculty members who might participate in walk-throughs as well? How do we follow up on walk-throughs?

_____

_____

_____

(Continued)

(Continued)

How do we ensure the safety of our students as they arrive at and depart from school?

_____

_____

_____

Which staff members are involved in this important supervision plan?

_____

_____

_____

My Visibility Checklist

☐ What is my current visibility plan?

☐ Where am I most visible?

☐ Where might I be more visible?

☐ What is distracting me from being more visible?

☐ How can I protect myself from distractions and interruptions?

☐ Am I doing frequent classroom walk-throughs?

☐ How often do I visit most classrooms?

☐ Which visible actions are done daily?

☐ Which visible actions are done weekly?

☐ Which visible actions are done monthly?

☐ How do I follow up with others after my "wandering around" activities?

☐ How many hours a day do I spend in my office?

☐ How might I reduce my "in-office" hours?

3

From Delegation to Collaboration

- Spread the Wealth
- Be the Bandleader
- Ask the Questions
- Empower Others

Strengths and Likes

To be a truly visible leader, as discussed in Chapter 2, you must be free from trying to do everything yourself. Each school is different, but most do have support staff for the principal, such as office assistants, counselors, deans, or assistant principals. The principal needs to be like an orchestra leader, orchestrating the goings-on of the players. This is where delegation comes into play. Delegation may be looked at as sharing the responsibilities necessary to create an exemplary school. A smart delegator will always look to the *strengths* of the team players. Who on your team is great with data interpretation? Who is a master of curriculum? Who has expertise in special education or English language learners? Who *likes* to work in the area of parent involvement? You may want to check out the delegation checklist at the end of this chapter.

Notice two key words in the above paragraph: *strengths* and *likes*. A team usually has players of varying abilities and interests. Just think for a moment of the players on your favorite sports teams. The good coach knows where to place and how to use his or her players. Look carefully at your people so as to make good matches. I was fortunate to have an assistant principal whose area of expertise was special education. She had taught students with learning disabilities before moving into administration and had worked with people with special needs in her personal life. She was the perfect person to be responsible for our exceptional student education department and curriculum. The teachers knew that not only did this administrator have experience and expertise in this area, she also had a love for her role. *Strengths* and *likes*: so important!

Strengths and *likes*: so important!

In *Happier*, Tal Ben-Shahar (2007) wrote, "Finding the right work—work that corresponds to both our passions and our strengths—can be challenging. We can begin the process by asking three crucial questions—what gives me meaning? What gives me pleasure? What are my strengths?" Continuing in this vane, Adam Bryant (2010), a *New York Times* columnist, interviewed Geoff Vuleta, CEO of Fahrenheit 212, an innovation consulting firm in Manhattan. Said Vuleta, "I try to uncover what people are really good at doing. . . . I never believed in obsessing over trying to get people to do things that they are no good at anyway." What a powerful statement!

I will talk about "celebration" in a later chapter, but I will mention here a counselor who took on a most important role, that of orchestrating our quarterly awards assembly while helping us celebrate. This man loved to recognize students for their accomplishments, and so prepared honor rolls in several different categories after each grading period. He then notified all the involved students and invited them to our assembly program, along with their families. What was really special were the beautifully prepared certificates with the students' names done in calligraphy on parchment paper and then laminated. My role as principal was to walk into the auditorium and receive the stack of certificates, stand at the podium, and call each student's name to come forward. Everyone in the school knew what this counselor did and appreciated him for his efforts and strong contribution to our program. He was a meticulous man who did his job to perfection and received much pleasure from a job well done. As Dwight Eisenhower, a five-star general and the thirty-fourth president of the United States said, "Leadership is the art of getting someone else to do something you want done because he wants to do it."

Delegation is really a builder of collaboration and needs to be a crucial focus for an education leader. When folks are working in harmony with a common vision in mind, and with a sharing of responsibilities, great things happen. Wikipedia defines collaboration as "working together to achieve a goal," and Henry Ford said, "If everyone is moving forward together, then success takes care of itself." Delegating should not be thought of as getting someone else to do your work but rather as a process to foster teamwork. Creating an exemplary school is all about having a vision and working as a team to achieve that. It is not about an almighty leader doing it all while others watch. Does your vision for success include meaningful collaboration?

I recall a principal colleague of mine who retired before her time because of what might be considered "burnout." She told me that all she did, day after day, was handle parent complaints and conduct parent conferences. Sound familiar? She did have a challenging school, but she had not taken the time to "share the wealth." Building a collaborative team would have turned things around for her. Unfortunately, her mind-set was that of "it's the leader's job to take care of all problems." If that were the case, why have support people at all?

> Delegation is really a builder of collaboration and needs to be a crucial focus for an education leader.

Delegating the smart way would mean that those closest to the issue would be the responsible persons. Parents may come to the school asking for the principal, but the bottom line is that they have issues to resolve. Who is best to resolve these issues? Might it be a teacher or a counselor or an assistant principal? Remember that the principal is the orchestra leader and as such cannot be tied to an office. Because my school was quite large, I had several assistant principals. Proper delegation was a most crucial leadership need for our school to run smoothly. As a principal new to the school, it was important for me to learn all I could about the staff. I had no history to rely on and was not familiar with the backgrounds of my support people. Two of the three assistant principals were new to the school as well, one being a brand new administrator.

Questioning

I will talk more about the significance of asking important questions, as opposed to issuing orders, in Chapter 7, on coaching, but in my case, it was the questioning that brought about a successful delegation plan. I asked my assistant principals where they felt their strengths and interests were. How did they see themselves helping the school? Where had they been successful in the past? What professional development had they recently been involved in? What brought them pleasure in past positions? Did they have a love for curriculum and what teachers were teaching? Did they enjoy visiting classrooms on a daily basis? How about data interpretation? How tech savvy were they? People indeed like to be asked about how they want to be involved. Those to whom you delegate want to have choices. Peter Drucker, world-renowned management guru and prolific author, said, "The leader of the past knew how to tell. The leader of the future will know how to ask."

Our school chose the route of assigning grade-level responsibilities to each assistant principal. This meant that one assistant principal might have overall responsibility for grades 6 and 7, while another might be in charge of the eighth grade plus English language learners. These assignments would rotate as the students moved from grade to grade, thus providing important continuity. A third assistant principal, as mentioned earlier, might have overall responsibility for those students in the exceptional education department. The teachers working within these grade-level areas would then have these particular administrators as part of their teams. In addition, parents knew whom to go to when they had concerns or questions regarding their children in a particular grade. It is possible that my previously mentioned colleague, who left the system early, might still be working in the profession she prepared for had she used a plan of smart delegation.

As we did with our assistant principals, we did with our counselors. Counselors were also assigned to particular grade levels and worked closely not only with their assistant principal but with their team leaders as well. There has been considerable conversation recently around the idea of dividing larger schools into smaller units, sometimes referred to as "houses" or "teams" or "academies." It is interesting to note that although this philosophy began in middle schools, because of its success, many high schools have also adopted it. Educators have observed that students often feel disconnected in large settings and that it is important for young people to have at least one adult with whom to relate within a school setting. Without actually setting out to do so, our plan of delegating specific areas of student responsibility to key support people led to the creation of a school-within-a-school concept. The resulting collaboration among the teachers, team leaders, counselors, and assistant principals provided a system whereby the needs of all students were met and the involvement of parents was enhanced.

Distribute the Wealth

In the March 2008 issue of the *Principal Leadership*, Kim Marshall's article "The Big Rocks: Priority Management for Principals" addresses delegation. What Kim says about delegating is as relevant today as it was in

2008. His message? "The goal is clear: teachers handling instruction and virtually all discipline problems, teacher teams using data to continuously improve teaching and learning, counselors preventing or dealing with students' emotional problems, custodians handling the physical plant, students taking increasing responsibility for their own learning, and the principal freed up to orchestrate the whole process" (p. 21).

> Delegation to those with the right strengths and interests is what it's all about.

In this era of high tech, most schools will find it necessary to have a staff member who is an expert in the field of technology. As we were getting ready to move "big time" into the area of computers in all classrooms, with e-mail communication for everyone, it was necessary to find a knowledgeable person to oversee this venture. Fortunately, one of our math teachers came forward with the expertise needed to assist in creating a state-of-the-art operation. Again, here was an individual with the strength and desire to do a great job. As I recall, I didn't go looking for him. He came to me with his proposal to be a part of our exciting new frontier. Again, collaboration and delegation, strength and interest, came into play. With a small master schedule adjustment, we were able to free this math teacher from one of his classes so that he would have the extra time to devote to his new responsibility. In a later chapter, when I talk about attendance improvement, I will share with you how this man, with his knowledge of programming, helped bring our student attendance to the top in the district. By the way, he didn't do this alone, but involved our attendance clerk and even me in this venture. Delegation to those with the right strengths and interests is what it's all about.

As a part of our process of delegating with collaboration as a goal, we had a wonderful and committed team of department heads and team leaders. These were teachers who might be referred to as teacher-leaders. They were, for the most part, teachers who had been at the school for several years and were eager to become involved with a new administration. The department heads took on the responsibility of ensuring that the proper curricula was in place for their particular disciplines and that books and materials were readily available. One of our assistant principals assumed the role of curriculum leader and therefore was the contact person for our department heads. Tom Peters, writer on management practices and coauthor of *In Search of Excellence* (Peters & Waterman, 2004), said, "Leaders don't create followers, they create more leaders." What a powerful thought!

Our team leaders also provided wonderful support and a complement to our department heads. Their role was to coordinate interdisciplinary units and to plan activities for their teams of teachers. In addition, these team leaders discussed any students presenting challenges to the teams during their regularly scheduled team meetings. In coordination with the grade-level counselors, the team leaders set up parent conferences, at which the involved teachers were present. Because parental involvement is usually a prominent goal at most schools, these meetings provided another avenue for achieving the goal.

Delegating the core elements of curriculum, as well as the management of student issues and the accompanying parental involvement, to school leaders enabled the school's administrative team to be involved in areas of management and supervision. Administrators were able to conduct daily classroom walk-throughs because they were not office-bound, handling student behavior issues or parent conferences. These often time-consuming activities were now mostly handled by the team leaders and the teacher teams. Clarence Otis, Jr., head of Darden Restaurants (Capital Grille, Olive Garden, Red Lobster, and Longhorn Steakhouse), believes in "getting the right people in place who have the talent and capability to get the work done and letting them do it."

I have been talking about strengths, and the importance of using the strengths of the core team. If we think about this concept for a moment, we should be able to realize that all of us really relish doing what we believe we are good at. If we are given a task we have to struggle with because we are just not "into it," we will not do the best job, and our real talents may be wasted. Marcus Buckingham and Donald Clifton wrote an excellent book titled *Now, Discover Your Strengths*. They wrote, "The value of the employee lies in their creativity, innovation, and good judgment. None of us, though, is creative, or innovative, or has good judgment in every single aspect of our work." Again, a reminder that the school leader is not the know-it-all, be-it-all, do-it-all genius of the school.

School-Based Management/Shared Decision Making

I believe that a crucial factor in the turnaround success of our school was the fact that everyone was involved in the mission of bringing about increased student achievement and a success for all philosophy. As Mark Goldberg (2001), author and high school principal, indicated in his *Lessons From Exceptional School Leaders*, "The era of the principal who must make all decisions and who, wittingly or not, treats teachers as if they have no capacity to make serious decisions is rapidly closing." Schools have to be like productive families. Everyone should have a role to play, and no one should be left out. There should be no secrets and no "favored children." Fortunately, when I was appointed principal, the district decided to pilot a new system of teacher involvement called School-Based Management (SBM)/Shared Decision Making (SBM/SDM), and our school was one of the few selected. Although the program was phased out under a subsequent superintendent, the principles embedded in the philosophy continued and have been replicated in whole or in part.

As the title indicated, under SBM, schools would have greater flexibility with hiring and budget, and under SDM, collaboration was king. For a principal, the idea of budgetary flexibility was exciting and challenging. It meant that a school had dollars based on student enrollment and that those dollars could be used at the discretion of the school, within legal restraints of course. This is where the SDM part of SBM/SDM came into play. A budget committee of interested faculty members was formed to discuss ways to appropriate our dollars that would best fit into our overall plan for school success. Did we want more teachers for smaller classes? Did we want fewer teachers with larger classes and more teacher assistants? Did we have a need for more technology?

Another area of SBM/SDM was that of personnel decisions, which previously were controlled by the principal, perhaps with involvement from the administrative team. A collaborative culture now called for participation on the part of teachers too. Our personnel committee was made up of those teachers who had an interest in interviewing prospective candidates and a grasp of our school's vision. In other words, they knew the type of teacher who would best fit the needs of our school. The committee was often joined by a teacher or two from the particular subject area involved.

> A collaborative culture now called for participation on the part of teachers too.

If we were interviewing for a social studies teacher, in addition to the committee members, there would be a teacher from that particular department. The committee would then present its recommendations to the principal.

It is interesting to note here that teachers were even involved in the hiring of the school's administrators. When an opening would come up for a new assistant principal, two teachers were selected to be on the interview committee, along with those individuals from the central office. In all the SBM/SDM pilot schools in the district, teachers were also on the interview panels to select the school's principal. Again, the rationale was that a school's faculty members would best understand the type of leader the school might require.

SBM/SDM, in addition to its budget and personnel committees, also included committees involved with curricular decisions, discipline issues, faculty social activities, and parental involvement. The curricular committee often looked at presentations of new textbook releases, discussed possible future course offerings, and planned testing schedules designed to be the least disruptive to the teaching and learning environment. It was this committee that discussed the need for a Gifted class for those students still in the English language learners program. Our school became the first to offer this class, which was taught by a teacher with a true passion for stimulating the minds of those students new to our country.

The discipline committee often looked at schoolwide situations that might need improvement. These might be issues not immediately apparent to school administrators. Those everyday problems faced by a large school, such as students in the halls at the wrong time and students not getting to school on time or being late to class, would often be topics for consideration. Additional security monitors were hired one year as a result of this committee's discussions and observations.

The social committee played a vital role in bringing about a positive school culture. Their interest revolved around creating happy events for all to share in. They planned the traditional holiday parties around Thanksgiving and Christmas but also looked for other areas for social involvement. Lunchtime events often were planned for National Hispanic Heritage Month and Black History Month. The committee did a wonderful job of delegating and collaborating by involving faculty members to help with special food preparation, decoration, and even entertainment. Often the band and chorus teachers were involved with their students. One year, because of our larger-than-usual Asian student population, an Asian luncheon was planned, catered by a neighborhood restaurant.

Parental involvement is certainly a crucial need for most schools and often presents a challenge. The parent committee worked on planning activities for parents that would be meaningful and beneficial for all. Social activities included coffees, pizza parties, and spaghetti dinners, while academic activities included ideas to help students with test preparation, how homework should be handled, and even computer literacy for parents, for which our computer lab would be open and available.

A very strong component of parental involvement, provided by our parent committee, was evening counseling sessions provided by one of our outstanding counselors. This counselor set aside one evening a week when she would conduct group counseling sessions on parenting skills as well as one-on-one meetings for those with special needs. Because ours was a Title I school, with a high percentage of low-income families, supplemental funding was provided. Because of this, we were able to hire a parent liaison coordinator, who worked closely with our parent committee in properly marketing our programs to the community.

Our SBM/SDM committees, along with our department leaders and team leaders, were truly the driving force toward our vision of creating an exemplary school. When thinking of the word "committee," I feel that the term does not truly reveal what these faculty groups were all about. Our committees were truly professional learning communities (PLCs), in that they were professionals working together for meaningful change and school improvement. Rich DuFour, a well-known educator, speaker, and author, is often associated with the PLC movement. In a May 2004 *Educational Leadership* article, he wrote that a PLC, among other things, could be a grade-level teaching team, a school committee, or a high school department. Attributes, according to an article in *Issues . . . About Change* (Hord, 1997–1998), include supportive and shared leadership, collective creativity, shared values and vision, supportive conditions, and shared personal practice.

One additional aspect of the SBM/SDM structure was the monthly open meeting, at which time the various PLCs presented updates as to their groups' activities over the previous month. Parents as well as students often attended, as did most of the faculty members. These meetings were held before school and always included a continental breakfast, sometimes accompanied by homemade items. The meetings provided transparency and fostered trust, as all could be part of the issues being considered as well as the initiatives being put in place.

Afterthoughts and Reflections

Who are my closest support people?

1. _____

2. _____

3. _____

4. _____

5. _____

What are their strengths?

1. _____

2. _____

3. _____

4. _____

5. _____

What are their roles?

1. _____

2. _____

3. _____

4. _____

5. _____

What might be a few of our top priorities for school improvement?

_____

_____

_____

Who might be interested in working on these projects?

_____

_____

_____

Whom can I call on to support our initiatives?

_____

_____

_____

Who might have been overlooked for leadership opportunities in the past?

_____

_____

_____

Who would like to organize and head up a PLC?

_____

_____

_____

Which parents or community members might like more involvement?

_____

_____

_____

Who is often voicing ideas and making suggestions?

_____

_____

_____

Who might like to switch roles?

_____

_____

_____

Which of our new faculty members might have been overlooked?

_____

_____

_____

(Continued)

(Continued)

Might we consider developing an SBM/SDM model?

_____

_____

_____

What committees would we include? Budget? Personnel?

_____

_____

_____

What advantages would this have for our school?

_____

_____

_____

Who would like to lead a group to research and discuss the topic?

_____

_____

_____

How am I helping create leaders?

_____

_____

_____

Am I asking more than telling?

_____

_____

_____

Check out:

http://www.marshallmemo.com

http://www.tmbc.com (Marcus Buckingham)

From Collaboration to Change

4

- Real and Lasting Change
- From Attendance to Blocks to Uniforms
- Building Teams

"**S**chool improvement" has been a buzzword for many years now. Most schools are required to produce school improvement plans on a yearly basis. These plans are often developed by school teams and are reviewed by a central office administrator. Too often, these plans are created to comply with district or state requirements and carry little weight after the completion and submission of the work. As important as continuous school improvement is to the success of a school, it must be a truly collaborative activity that will lead to real change. School improvement, by its very definition, means that only by change will things improve, and yes, we all know that change is not easy. There are probably more leadership books written about effecting change than most any other topic.

Kenneth A. Sirotnik and Richard W. Clark (1988), in the *Phi Delta Kappan*, wrote, "The ultimate power to change is—and always has been—in the heads, hands, and hearts of the educators who work in the schools. Decisions must be made where the action is." Following this line of thought, put forward by a research professor and a school superintendent, we can see that collaboration is the foundation of change. Change comes about when those involved

> Collaboration is the foundation of change.

believe in what the proposed change will do for the school's mission. Change comes about when there is true involvement by all parties. Real meaningful and sustainable change does not come about when it is imposed from above. Teachers, especially, are tired of having new and different systems imposed upon them, only to be replaced in a few years.

Attendance Improvement

My very first change initiative, as a principal interested in turning around an unacceptable situation, was to improve overall student attendance. Most schools have attendance improvement as one of their goals for several reasons. First of all, in most cases, funds to the schools are involved. States forward money to schools on the basis of average daily student attendance or similar formulas. Second, and perhaps most important, students cannot learn if they are not in school. Third, many school rating systems include student attendance as one of the markers of success. Also, many schools spend considerable time, energy, and money tracking students with numerous absences that might be labeled truancies.

Miami-Dade County Public Schools publishes a listing after each grading period, which ranks all schools on the basis of their average daily student attendance. This listing is divided into one for elementary schools, one for middle schools, one for high schools, and one for special centers. The document is sent, via school mail, to all schools, regional offices, district offices, and board members. It is a very visible indication of which schools are doing a good job bringing students into school and, of course, which schools are failing in this crucial area. As I recall, this attendance document was one of the very first items I saw as I assumed my new role as principal. As I read the

> Might attendance improvement be my very first attempt at real school change using a collaborative model?

rankings, I could not help but be disappointed when I saw that my new school was ranked thirty-eighth among fifty middle schools in the district. Might attendance improvement be my very first attempt at real school change using a collaborative model? Would not an improvement in overall student attendance be a very visible way of showing that turnaround was indeed taking place?

When I began talking with our attendance clerk, and with a counselor, and a few staff members who had been at the school for a while, I learned that poor attendance was a given. Students were not expected to attend regularly, the staff informed me, because of the culture of the families. The mostly Hispanic families were very protective and would keep their children home if the weather was not just right. If a younger child in the family was ill, an older child might be kept home while a parent went to work. If a child had a doctor or dentist appointment, the child would take the entire day off from school. When a parent had an appointment of any kind, the child would accompany the parent, often to serve as a translator. School was not a top priority, and the value of regular daily attendance was not appreciated by families or students.

After listening to all the reasons preventing our school from being one of the top schools in attendance in the district, I sat down with our attendance clerk and a counselor and an assistant principal to talk about possible things we could do to turn around the obviously unacceptable attendance issue. Our school had been doing the usual routine procedures, such as making phone calls to absentees' homes, sending letters to homes after numerous absences, having counselors meet with students with excessive absences, and even sending the school visiting teacher/social worker to the homes. As a last resort, referrals to juvenile court were made. These procedures had been in place for many years but failed to remedy the problem of high student absenteeism. Obviously a new plan was needed.

The plan decided upon was to be a competition among the homerooms to see which class would have the highest percentage of attendance and would therefore be eligible for certain rewards. Most students are excited about competing, and we soon learned that teachers are too. Our plan was simple: As the principal, I would announce each day, during morning announcements, those homerooms with 100 percent attendance the previous day. Every Monday, I would announce the top homerooms at each grade level for the previous week. At the end of each grading period, usually nine weeks, the top homeroom at each grade level would be rewarded with a field trip of their choice to a local tourist attraction, movie, park, or game spot.

The competition proved to be a great motivating factor for all, with teachers often becoming the most competitive. We would even hear stories of a teacher calling one absent student to say that he or she was breaking the class's 100 percent record and, if at all possible, please come to school. Students knew too that their attendance was important to help maintain the competitive edge for their homeroom classmates and teachers. The excitement grew when a grading period came to an end and the winners were announced. The grade-level assistant principal would always visit the winning classes and discuss with them their choices for field trip rewards.

Often, community groups or local businesses would help us in our improvement efforts. One of our most exciting and successful competitions was when the Miami Heat basketball team initiated a districtwide middle school competition. Any student with perfect attendance for a complete nine-week grading period would receive free admission to a special game, along with a chance to meet the players. The excitement was high at our school, and students began to realize that they could come to school on a daily basis and profit from it.

A neighboring high school was fortunate to partner with a prominent local car dealership, which provided many incentives throughout the school year to encourage good attendance. The really big prize, which resulted in a feature story in the local newspaper, was a brand-new car awarded to a graduating senior with perfect attendance. Students, whether they are elementary, middle, or senior high, are truly motivated by competitions and rewards.

As an additional component of our plan, if the entire school maintained 95 percent or better in daily attendance, from Monday to Thursday, the students were rewarded with permission to wear shorts on Friday. This was quite a big deal to the students, because our school required that uniforms be worn daily. To be able to wear shorts, especially in Miami, was a great motivator, and the students came to realize that this reward was a true group effort. On Thursday of each week, as students entered the cafeteria, they would enthusiastically ask if tomorrow would be a shorts day. This became such a ritual that one of our teachers made a clip-on badge for me to wear that read, "Yes, Tomorrow is Shorts Day." If I was not in the building on a Thursday, one of our assistant principals would wear the sign. Traditions and rituals are important.

The results were truly amazing. Each quarter, we could see our climb up the attendance ladder. Our attendance clerk would take great pride in bringing the district report to my office and placing it atop my daily school mail. She knew she was appreciated, as she was a big part of our accomplishments because of her unwavering focus on home phone calls. I would always announce the quarterly standings to the entire school. We all took great pride in seeing our school rise to the top twenty and then the top ten, and finally, one quarter, to number one in the district.

We had a big celebration for our number one standing. Our cafeteria manager made chocolate chip cookies for all the students, and I took great pride in presenting one to each student as they picked up their lunch. We also had a large marquee in the front of the school, where we posted our big news. Additionally, we rented a large helium balloon with a banner reading "We are #1" and had it mounted above the school auditorium.

> We had a big celebration for our number one standing.

School pride, which had been more or less nonexistent in prior years, now came to the forefront. Being recognized for our achievement in increasing student attendance, and of course for being number one, gave everyone a reason to be proud of our school. I can still recall seeing a student in the mall, who had been at our school several years prior, asking me if we were still number one. Pride is a powerful motivator, and pride in one area can lead to pride in other areas as well.

Collaboration definitely led to real and meaningful change. Yes, the students and their parents did their part. The whole community knew about our efforts to show that attendance matters. Of course, the teachers played a major role by motivating and promoting our initiative. The attendance clerk was invaluable. Substitute teachers even volunteered to help with phone calls on their off time, and I as the principal made many a call

> Pride is a powerful motivator, and pride in one area can lead to pride in other areas as well.

when my work day might have been over. As Dean Acheson, an American statesman, once said, "Always remember that the future comes one day at a time."

A really major behind-the-scenes part of our attendance improvement effort was our technology expert/math teacher/middle school coordinator. He was the man who designed a computer program that recorded the daily attendance of every homeroom in the school. He received the list daily from the attendance clerk and inputted the data. Over the weekend, on his own time, he and his program computed the standings for the week. Each Monday morning, he walked into my office with the rankings prepared for me to read during the morning announcements.

Parent Report Card Pickup

All schools, whether urban, rural, suburban, elementary, or secondary, have to deal with reporting to parents on the progress of their students. Schools often experiment with what might be the most effective manner in which to do this. Many schools send report cards home with students and ask that they be signed by the parents and returned to the schools. This is often a burdensome procedure for teachers. Some schools mail report cards home, but this can be costly, and there is no assurance that parents received them. Today, many schools are using online methods of grade reporting, which may be a move forward providing that all or most families have Internet access and reliable computers.

We started what proved to be a unique and meaningful process of report card distribution, which we called parent report card pickup. The program was simple in that parents were invited to come to school to receive their children's report cards after each grading period. To accommodate varied parent schedules, we provided an evening and morning schedule. Parents who were available in the morning came in on a Wednesday from 7 to 9 a.m. Parents who preferred an evening came to the school between 4 and 7 p.m. on a Tuesday. Notices and e-mails were distributed in advance, and an announcement was displayed on the front-of-school marquee. Those parents who could not make either one of our pickup times could come into the school office at any time after the official days to retrieve the report card.

The entire process took place in the school media center/library, with areas designated for each grade level. The grade-level tables were manned by teachers, on a rotating basis, from each particular grade. Counselors were present, as were the members of the administrative team. As an additional ingredient, members of the school chorus or jazz band would often perform. Refreshments were available as well.

Not only was this program a very effective report card distribution process, but it also was a wonderful parental involvement event. It is often felt that some parents, especially those not used to the American system of education, are reluctant to visit their children's schools. They may not know what to expect or what might be expected of them. Knowing that report card pickup was a crucial part of their children's progress, and that this was really their role as parents, seemed to set a favorable tone. Often families came as units, with grandparents and siblings attending as well. Report card pickup became a tradition.

The scene at pickup time was quite rewarding to observe: Parents and families entering and exiting and socializing with one another and with staff members. Parents asking questions of the teachers seated at the tables and of the counselors and administrators. Parents and students jointly viewing the report card grades. Most families leaving with smiles on their faces and others talking in earnest with their children's counselors or assistant principals. Older siblings, now in high school, renewing relationships with former teachers, and younger siblings thinking eagerly of their future middle school careers.

Conversion to Middle School

Our school had been a junior high school throughout its long history, with a grade configuration of grades 7 through 9. Most school systems in the United States operated under a system of elementary school, junior high school, and high school. Research was beginning to show that there was a need for a different type of experience at the junior high school level. The National Middle School Association (now the Association for Middle Level Education) began promoting a more personal and relevant format for young adolescents, to include advisory programs, teams, and exploratory offerings. Miami-Dade County Public Schools decided to become a part of this movement, as was most of the country, which meant converting all of its fifty junior high schools into middle schools. When I arrived at Palm Springs, the lettering on the building still read "Junior High School."

Delegating fosters collaboration, which facilitates change. That was my belief. By involving others as a team, we were all a part of this change effort. It was not a top-down mandate but a buy-in from all involved. It was obvious that this conversion from a junior high to a middle school, with all that it entailed, would be a major undertaking. To make it a more difficult task, there was no room for the ninth graders to move to the high school, as the neighborhood high schools were already over-crowded. That meant that we would be bringing in sixth graders and keeping ninth graders, all while creating a meaningful middle school experience for all.

> Delegating fosters collaboration, which facilitates change. That was my belief.

We started by assembling a cadre of teachers who were eager to bring about long-awaited change. They knew the school had not been successful. The proof was in the dismal attendance record, the high failure rate and subsequent retentions, the high teacher turnover rate, and the unfavorable standing in the community. Teachers were asked to volunteer for the role of team leader. We decided that two team leaders for each grade level would be the model that would accommodate all of our students. From that point, after delegating leadership responsibilities to our team leaders, teachers were selected to be on one of the newly formed teams. The team structure would include a teacher from each of the core academic areas: language arts, mathematics, science, and social studies, plus one or two elective teachers.

Our school was unique in that it did have a ninth grade, which technically was not a middle school grade, and it also had a large population of students learning English for speakers of other languages. Additionally, there were many students considered to be part of our exceptional student education department, which included students with varying learning disabilities as well as those considered to qualify for the district's Gifted program. Meeting with our core group of middle school planners, we decided to create teams with these special groups in mind. Our ninth grade teachers were pleased to be a part of the transformation to middle school, so the entire school was united around our new and innovative program. It is interesting to note that the middle school team approach was so well received in many quarters that it was later adopted by many high schools.

Collaboration does indeed facilitate change, and our collaborative process brought about a whole new way of structuring our school and serving our students. Now, instead of teachers' teaching in isolation, they were working as teams and planning interdisciplinary units of instruction. Our administrative team developed a schedule to facilitate meeting times. Three thirty-minute periods a week, before the student day began, were set aside for team meetings. It was during these times that the teachers could plan together, discuss specific students, and even meet with parents. As visible administrators, I and our assistant principals enjoyed walking through the building during these meeting times and hearing the team discussions or "putting in our two cents."

> Collaboration does indeed facilitate change, and our collaborative process brought about a whole new way of structuring our school and serving our students.

Hopefully, everything we do at a school will lead to improved student achievement. We were confident that our new middle school plan would do just that. Teacher teams were collaborating on teaching units with support from subject-area department heads. All teams chose a team name and a mascot. This was a collaborative student activity; a lesson in the democratic process. Our middle school coordinator, the same man who taught math and was our tech person and the developer of our computerized attendance program, took on the job of providing material for our advisory program. He wore many hats, as did so many of our faculty members. People do want to be involved in what is happening, especially when their views are listened to and when the school's leadership is inclusive.

As an additional step in our conversion process, in year 2, we did a complete room change, so that teams could be centered in the same area, either across the hall or next door to each other. Asking teachers to move from a classroom they may have called "home" for a number of years to a new room is not an easy ask. However, we all knew that grouping teams together was a vital part of middle school. I had been providing the faculty with articles on successful middle schools, and our professional development activities always centered around middle school implementation. In addition, many of our teachers had been provided the opportunity to attend workshops and conferences on the middle school philosophy.

A quick Amazon search of books about change reveals that there are over 52,000 listings on change alone, with 39,000 under change management, and 30,000 under school change. Obviously this is a "hot" topic and one that presents problems for many school leaders. Two of my colleagues have written books themselves on change: Dr. Lew Smith's (2008) *Schools That Change* and Karla Reiss's (2012) *Be a Changemaster*. Lew outlines what it took for eight schools to win his annual School Change Award competition, and Karla provides strategies for overcoming resistance to change. I believe that our change to a middle school came about for two main reasons: teachers realized that their school was not meeting with success, and they were personally involved in bringing about the desired change.

Promoting a Block Schedule

If we believe that changing the way people do things is challenging, and we all agree it is, think for a moment about what it was like to change the way the school day was structured for some 1,800 students and 100-plus teachers. Routines are particularly hard to change, especially if they are routines that have been carried out for years and perhaps decades. Well, we did make the change, as an enhancement to our middle school program and as a strategy for increasing student achievement. We often hear about the significance of time on task in helping students learn, yet most schools operate on a schedule of fifty minutes per subject. When you subtract time for roll taking, announcements, review, and homework preparation, the actual academic time on task loses an additional ten minutes. Our schedule had included six periods per day, plus a homeroom/advisory period, with time built in for lunch. Now we were going to move to three periods a day while doubling the length of each class, thus greatly increasing time on task.

To begin this major transformation, we first had to begin discussions about what a block schedule is, how it might work in our school, what benefits it might provide, what the downside might be, and of course what the current literature was saying about block scheduling. Our faculty had heard about this type of schedule through our work in the conversion from junior high to middle school. Most of our faculty members had attended workshops and conferences as part of middle school professional development activities, so they had been exposed to the varying block schedule models.

Our administrative team was all in favor of the positive effects this new schedule would bring, so we began conversations with our department heads and our team leaders. We shared research and articles on scheduling with them and listened to their thoughts. These school leaders then talked with their teams and departments. At the start of the second paragraph of this chapter, I referred to change involving the head, heart, and hands. Well, this was the "head" part: let's all understand what a block schedule can do for our students' learning and how it might facilitate improved teaching as well. Our bimonthly faculty meetings provided additional opportunities for learning about block scheduling.

Fortunately, there were a few middle schools in our district that had already begun operating with block schedules, and they were receptive to a team of our teachers visiting their schools. In addition, some of our teachers had seen the block schedule in action through visits during conferences they had attended. I can still recall the excitement and enthusiasm exhibited by our returning visitation team after seeing a neighboring school actually functioning under this new format. They were ready to start and to share what they had observed with the rest of the faculty. Looking back at "head, heart, and hands," this would have to be the "heart" part. The visitation team had truly become emotionally involved in thinking about what this new idea could do for our school.

It probably is not wise to "jump into" something as major as a complete restructuring of the school day, along with the way teachers teach and plan lessons, and the way students interact with the learning process. We decided, as a school, to do a trial run for one grading period and then to conduct a simple vote afterward. This was a

This was the "hands" part of our "head, heart, and hands" formula.

wise decision for many reasons, most important, to bring along those teachers who were still "on the fence" as well as those teachers who did not like the plan at all. Everyone was willing to try something new, as long as it was a trial run and would be evaluated at the end. This was the "hands" part of our "head, heart, and hands" formula. If the vote was favorable for continuing, the new schedule would be implemented the following school year.

The block schedule we implemented consisted of three classes a day. These classes rotated so that they would meet every other day. All students had six classes, so the division was simple. Day 1 would be periods 1, 3, and 5, and day 2 would be periods 2, 4, and 6: an odd-period day followed by an even-period day. To add an extra, rather unique feature, the periods rotated within the day.

Block Schedule

A	B	C	D	E	F
1	2	3	4	5	6
3	4	5	6	1	2
5	6	1	2	3	4

The above table shows a cycle of six days. When the cycle is completed, it starts over again. Students would have attended all six classes in a two-day period, with all classes rotating from the first block to the middle block to the last block. As an example, my period 1 class might be math, and that would meet during the first block on Monday (A). On Wednesday (C), my math class would meet during the last block, and on Friday (E), it would meet during the middle block.

The overwhelming majority of teachers voted to make our new schedule a part of our school day for the upcoming school year. Our technology/middle school coordinator took on the job of preparing the schedule in calendar form for the entire school year. These schedules were printed in the students' daily planners, were posted on bulletin boards around the school, and were visible on our website as well. Although appearing a bit confusing to me at first, everything moved like clockwork. The teachers settled into working through longer class periods and appreciated the opportunity to have their planning periods at different times of the day.

Students needing extra help found the expanded time to be a great benefit. Students were not checking the clock to see how much time they had left. Classes seemed to be more relaxed knowing that the change-of-class bell would not be sounding just as they were settling into their work. Science classes, as well as most elective classes, easily profited from having sufficient time to complete activities. Meeting at different times of the day allowed students to perform at their best learning times. An additional positive outcome was the fact that the school was quieter and calmer because student movement was decreased by 50 percent.

Uniforms for All

A final collaborative effort, leading to major change, was our conversion from a moderate student dress code to one of school uniforms. Actually, this came about through a district initiative to move all schools to mandatory uniforms. Wisely, the process of altering the school's dress code was left to each school's discretion, as long as there was parental involvement along with a voting procedure. Our school convened a committee consisting of an administrator, several teachers, parents, and students. This committee looked at various uniform styles and colors, with samples provided by local school uniform companies. Selections were made, with options given to students to vote upon.

This was truly a collaborative effort, involving students, administrators, teachers, and parents. Although our students, being typical early adolescents, were not happy with the idea of giving up their jeans and wearing uniforms, they did understand the democratic process. The overall voting resulted in affirming the move to school uniforms. Students had a choice of blue or beige for pants and skirts, and blue, white, or beige for shirts. The shift went smoothly, beginning in the following school year, with very few dissenters. The district provided an option for parents to opt out if they had strong objections, but very few did.

Afterthoughts and Reflections

Are we following our school improvement plan?

_____

_____

_____

What might be the top three most significant aspects of our plan?

_____

_____

_____

Are we all on the same path?

_____

_____

_____

What changes or modifications might we make?

_____

_____

_____

Is the plan producing the changes we are hoping for?

_____

_____

_____

What changes have we actually realized this school year?

_____

_____

_____

Are there strategies to be put in place to improve student attendance?

_____

_____

_____

(Continued)

(Continued)

Have we considered the importance of school pride?

_____

_____

_____

What programs are in place to build pride in our students and in our school?

_____

_____

_____

Can we enhance team building among our teachers?

_____

_____

_____

Are our professional learning communities functioning satisfactorily?

_____

_____

_____

How about our master schedule? Is it serving the needs of our students?

_____

_____

_____

Does our student dress code need revision?

_____

_____

_____

Supporting Students at Risk

- Appropriate Education for All
- Harvard Recognition
- SARP and SCSI
- Save the Arts

Meeting the needs of all students has always been a challenge for schools. The goal for schools should be success for all. The No Child Left Behind legislation was intended to ensure that schools focus on the achievement of all students assigned to them. Many years ago, schools were designed around "tracks." This meant that some students were on track to attend college, while other students were in programs to prepare for occupations only requiring a high school diploma. Today there is much talk about students being "college ready." Our world seems to be changing so quickly that it is difficult to know what students will really need to know in the future.

Public schools are required by law to provide an appropriate education for students who have been identified as having certain learning challenges. Our school attempted to meet the academic and social-emotional needs of students classified as learning disabled, emotionally handicapped, autistic, and deaf or hard of hearing. Teachers needed special certification to work with special education students, and there were specific courses designed to meet the needs of these students. Students who were classified as Gifted after being tested also qualified for special classes taught by teachers who had received special training.

English language learners were another group of students who required unique classes taught by teachers who had received training in teaching English as a second language. Our school also had a large population of students who were newly arrived to the United States from Cuba as well as other Spanish-speaking countries. Again, as with exceptional student education, federal laws indicated how these students would be serviced.

It would appear from reading the above paragraphs that all students were indeed being provided with appropriate education programs that would ensure that they would meet with success. Unfortunately, this was not the case historically in our school, and it is apparently not the case in most of the nation's schools. There is a population of students often referred to as "at risk" or potential "dropouts." We read continually in the newspapers and hear on TV news reports about the student drop-out problem. Yet educators have not been able to find a suitable solution. The mandated state testing program has proved to be an obstacle to graduation for so many of the nation's at-risk population.

PBS's *Frontline* ran an episode on September 25, 2012, titled "Dropout Nation" (Koughan & Vargas, 2012). The program featured one high school in Houston, Texas, that was representative of what were referred to as "drop-out factories." The school, Sharpstown High School, was working diligently to find ways to reach all of its potential drop-out population. Despite a staff of dedicated professionals, it is still proving a difficult task, when students' home lives are often in complete disarray.

Breaking Schools' Rules

In 2011, a major study was released by the Council of State Governments Justice Center titled Breaking Schools' Rules. This was a six-year study that traced 1 million secondary students in Texas. The results of the study pointed to the fact that there were too many students being suspended or expelled, often numerous times, for infractions that might have been handled in ways leading to positive outcomes. The report's message suggests that these routine punishments often create a pipeline leading from student retention to far too many suspensions and expulsions to joblessness and, for a considerable number of unskilled young people, to prison. Many politicians have begun to refer to the problem of at-risk students as the civil rights issue of our century.

If we, as educators, truly believe that all students can learn, and that all children should have an appropriate education, then we must do whatever is necessary to ensure success for all. We were fortunate at Palm Springs Middle School to realize that the needs of too many students were not being met. We could no longer say that their failures were their own fault or the fault of their parents or home life. We could no longer place blame on the elementary school or the previous year's teacher. We had to, as a collaborative group, come up with a plan of action that would suit our population and would result in a quality and equal education for all groups.

> Many politicians have begun to refer to the problem of at-risk students as the civil rights issue of our century.

The Birth of a New Program

Perhaps because I had been a school counselor, with a master's degree in guidance and counseling, before entering school administration, I was appalled by the large number of neglected students at my new school. There were literally hundreds of students who had been retained one or more years because of excessive absences, failing grades in classes, and unacceptable behavior often leading to school suspensions. This pattern had become embedded in the culture of the school. Just as folks believed that poor student attendance was to be expected in our neighborhood, they also believed that failure in school for a large population of students was to be expected.

Fortunately, I found other student-oriented faculty members who would join me in attempting to reverse this completely unacceptable situation. "All students can learn" was a much used phrase in education circles, but it was not really believed in many schools. The separation of "haves and have-nots" would need to stop. Students could not continue to fail in such overwhelming numbers if we were to turn Palm Springs Middle School into a successful learning environment for all students.

Collaborating with several counselors and teacher leaders indicated that there was certainly a need to find a way to turn around our failing student population. Not only should this effort be a top priority, but it really couldn't be put on the "back burner." When teachers began hearing talk about positive plans for our most challenging population, they actually became excited. Most teachers had several students in each of their classes who could be problematic because of behavior issues. Most behavior problems came about because these students were struggling with academic deficiencies, and having to repeat a grade did not help the situation. Relieving teachers of some of their most difficult students was music to their ears.

As has been mentioned previously, there were programs for special education students, for English language learners, and for Gifted students. Where were the special programs for the identified at-risk students, along with special classes and special teachers? Was there a need for an additional designation or classification? Could we really build a great school while neglecting the needs of this special group? After many conversations, and formal and informal meetings, we decided on a new venture labeled SARP: the Student at Risk Program.

> Where were the special programs for the identified at-risk students, along with special classes and special teachers?

Teachers, in their team meetings, were asked to identify their most challenging students. These were to be students who were experiencing difficulty in academic areas. Students who were poor readers, as well as those deficient in math skills. Students who had been retained and were repeating a grade but still were struggling. And of course those students who could be labeled "disruptive" because of behavior problems often caused by falling behind academically. These identified "at-risk" students would become our very first members of SARP.

We started with 100 students in grades 7 and 8, who would now be their own SARP team. Being a Title I school, designated as such because of our high percentage of low-income families, we did have funds for additional personnel. One of the first things we did was to add a counselor, who was already a member of our staff and had just earned her certification. This counselor met with our prospective SARP students and their parents to explain what this new opportunity might offer them. They would have smaller classes, along with increased individual attention, and they would be provided with close counselor support. The team of teachers would be made up of a teacher for each of the four core subjects—math, language arts, science, and social studies—plus a paraprofessional, a counselor, and a team leader.

We were fortunate in that the district had just completed a major construction project for our school, which included a four-pack: a building with just four classrooms and an office. This provided a perfect area for our SARP team and could even be considered a "school within a school," which was a common theme in school improvement rhetoric. Students did not have to leave their special area when classes changed except to go to their elective classes and lunch. The five minutes between classes was a time for casual interaction between students and teachers.

The teachers selected to be SARP teachers really were volunteers for the most part. All schools have a cadre of teachers who especially like working with challenging students, are good at understanding the needs of this special group, and are liked and respected by the students. It is often said that people enter the teaching profession because they want to help young people. Being a SARP teacher would certainly fulfill this desire.

SARP was a true "win-win" situation. Previously neglected students were now being supported both academically and emotionally. The teachers knew that their students were in need of remediation. They also knew that their students needed much encouragement, as well as supportive feedback. The teachers knew that they could not give up on their new charges. And the students had, possibly for the first time in their educational careers, a feeling of family. They all belonged to SARP. They were not outsiders anymore, but belonged to a team of students and teachers and caring adults who all had as their goal "success for all."

> SARP was a true "win-win" situation. Previously neglected students were now being supported both academically and emotionally.

The other aspect of our win-win situation was that the teachers in our regular program now had classes without the previous challenging student population. This allowed teachers to completely focus their instruction without the distraction of providing for students who presented rather severe learning and behavior issues. It was now possible for a teacher to provide assistance to those who might have been passed over because of concentration on disruptive students.

Behavior issues were so greatly reduced that our assistant principals finally had time to provide support to teachers. The SARP team members handled almost all unacceptable student behavior among themselves. Their teachers were understanding of the needs of this special population, and the in-house counselor was always on call. Teachers in the regular program now had very few behavioral issues, and

> Behavior issues were so greatly reduced that our assistant principals finally had time to provide support to teachers.

the few they had were handled as a team. Sending students to the principal's office became a thing of the past. Administrators increased their mentoring of new teachers through increased time for informal classroom observations. Curricular issues were handled expeditiously, and teachers knew that their assistant principals were ready partners.

A final significant segment of our SARP was the inclusion of parents on a greater scale than previously. First of all, all SARP parents came to the school for an initial placement conference. Those parents who were not able to come to the school were visited at their homes or even their places of work by the team leader. All parents knew what this new program would be about and what it could do for their children. We asked for parents to assist us by making sure their children were in school every day and that they spent some academic time at home nightly.

When necessary, parents were called in for early-morning team meetings to discuss issues of concern. In addition, there were frequent evening parent education programs specifically designed to meet the needs of our SARP parents. Not all parent activities were focused on academics. The team enjoyed putting together luncheons for the parents, with students and teachers doing all the preparations. These luncheons often centered on certain holidays, like Mother's Day, and were always enjoyed by everyone.

Very few students failed a grade anymore. Some students were actually promoted, as a result of extra credit earned, to the grades in which they would have been had they not been retained. The entire school showed a dramatic decrease in the number of students needing to repeat a grade. Emphasis was now put on success, not failure. As a principal, I reviewed each teacher's quarterly grades and did a grade analysis so that teachers would be aware of the passing rates of students in their classes. Counselors were able to provide interventions for students who might be struggling in particular subjects. Title I funds provided for after-school tutoring for students needing extra support.

Electives to the Rescue

There has been a trend in recent years to consider eliminating certain elective courses, such as music, art, and physical education. The thinking behind this is that students need to spend more time on the core academic subjects. In many cases, students are required to "double up" on classes such as reading and math because of deficiencies they have exhibited. Very often, these students have failed to pass state-mandated tests. The hope is that more time on task will remedy the failing situation. In addition, many school districts struggle with decreased funding from the state and look at eliminating nonrequired subjects from their offerings as a way to cut costs.

Our school was fortunate in having very strong music, art, vocational, and physical education teachers who would have been quite distraught at the thought of losing their programs. They were true believers in the benefits of nonacademic offerings in rounding out a child's education. Most significantly, our music and art programs were the most popular classes in the school. We had a full band program, including an outstanding jazz band, plus a full chorus program. Two art teachers, with full classes, rounded out our fine arts program.

Elective offerings actually saved many of our at-risk students from becoming dropouts. We discovered that many of our students who were having difficulty in academic areas really had significant talent in the arts. It is not a secret that young people love their music and often long to be part of a musical group. To take this opportunity away from them only turns them off to education more quickly. Indeed, the participation of our at-risk students in music and art was a true motivating force behind their desire to be a part of our school and to be successful as well. It was a rewarding experience for our faculty to observe a musical performance featuring students who were now succeeding academically, in great part because of their participation in something they truly loved.

Many students have a creative streak, and we had our share of creative students, including those who believed themselves to be graffiti artists. Often we would arrive at school, after a weekend, and find that a graffiti artist had been at work decorating a back wall of our building. Often our custodial crew could clean it up. Sometimes we would have to call the district's paint department to paint over the graffiti. Knowing which of our students were involved encouraged us to invite them to paint a graffiti-style mural on a prominent wall in one of our outside hallways. I even took them to Home Depot to purchase their paint cans. Needless to say, these students were as proud as could be of their work and could not have been more appreciative of the opportunity provided by their school. Art, as well as music, can be a powerful force in keeping students in school.

Sports are often a big part of a student's life, and the opportunity to be a part of school athletics has always been a big draw. We were fortunate to have a strong physical education department and an active student body, so our physical education classes were usually filled. Again, this was a place where students could excel when possibly they could not in academic areas. They also had the opportunity to participate in after-school intermural competitions. The idea was to help all students be connected in some way.

The key to our success with students deemed to be possible future school dropouts was providing them with opportunities to become truly involved in school life. These were the same students who might have been excluded from school life in the past. Exclusion breeds contempt and further isolation, and becomes a downward spiral. Providing academic classes that allowed success became the foundation of our drop-out prevention program, upon which further opportunities could be built. As a faculty, we looked for opportunities to open doors for all of our students. A closed door to a young person very often says "You are not wanted here."

> The idea was to help all students be connected in some way.

School Center for Special Instruction

There was a second major component, along with SARP, which helped greatly with our commitment to put the drop-out problem behind us, and that was our School Center for Special Instruction (SCSI). This was actually a district program with funds provided to schools for the hiring of an SCSI position. We were fortunate to have a faculty member who felt strongly about saving students from becoming school dropouts. Again, we need to keep in mind the importance of delegating to those with strengths and interests in the particular area. This man had the personality and talents needed to be successful with a most difficult population.

SCSI was what might be considered a last-chance opportunity for students who might otherwise be removed from school, through the suspension or expulsion process. It was actually an alternative to suspension. Many schools often resort to suspending students from school for various infractions of school rules. Reasons for suspension might be such things as disrespect to teachers, use of unacceptable language, failure to cooperate, fighting, and even truancy. Suspensions often lasted from a few days to as many as ten days out of school. Expulsions would be for repeat offenders and could last as long as a school year. Unfortunately, the very students needing the most in-school time are often the ones being removed from the learning environment. It becomes a cycle that puts at-risk students further and further behind and becomes a highway to dropping out of school.

The SCSI operated as a self-contained classroom. It was a small room with a capacity of approximately twelve students. Students were assigned there by school administrators when it was determined that they had to be removed from the normal class setting for a period of time ranging from three to ten days. Students spent the entire school day as SCSI students and were responsible for completing regular classroom assignments, along with any other assignments given by the SCSI instructor. Because of the small number of students in SCSI at any given time, often as few as three or four, the instructor was able to establish a quality relationship with each student and could provide counseling as well.

For many students, their SCSI time was a turnaround experience for them. They realized that this was a last-chance opportunity, but it was not what might be considered the "end of the road." The students had a chance to take a hard look at where they had gone wrong and what they might need to do academically and socially in the future. Being in one classroom with one teacher, who has your interests at heart, all day long for several days, can be an altering experience. Although some students were repeat offenders and were assigned to SCSI more than once, most students truly profited from their one-on-one time and knew that they had indeed been given another chance.

Harvard Study

Palm Springs Middle School was well on its way to truly becoming a school where all students would be successful. Students with learning challenges were well served in our exceptional student education program. English language learners were instructed in our English for speakers of other languages program, while other students were provided special instruction through our Gifted program. With our new SARP, along with the SCSI, we were hopeful and optimistic, believing that we could now be a school that truly met the needs of all students.

It was a rewarding surprise when we were contacted by The Civil Rights Project of Harvard University to be featured as a success story in a report they were compiling titled *Opportunities Suspended: The Devastating Consequences of Zero Tolerance and School Discipline* (The Civil Rights Project, Harvard University, 2000). The researchers studied the various philosophies used by different principals in four Miami-Dade middle schools. How discipline problems were handled was a major focus, along with the use of suspension in handling unacceptable behavior. In the schools studied, the suspension rate ranged from below 2 percent to more than 42 percent. Our school sat at 3.4 percent.

The report, which was presented as part of the National Summit on Zero Tolerance in Washington, D.C., in the summer of 2000, highlighted the programs Palm Springs Middle School had put in place to assist potential student dropouts. The report referred to Comer and Poussaint's (1992) book *Raising Black Children*, in which it was stressed that discipline should not be used as a punishment or means of control, but as a way to help a child solve a problem, develop inner controls, and learn better ways of expressing feelings. This was truly the Palm Springs Middle School philosophy, held by the majority of our faculty members.

One of our successful programs, which was also mentioned in the Harvard study, was HeartSmarts. This program was a product of the Institute of HeartMath of California and helped students focus on their hearts when dealing with stressful situations. The program taught communication skills, strategies to distinguish between intelligent choices and emotional impulses, and how to deal with anger and stress. HeartSmarts was discovered by one of our counselors while attending a conference and became so popular that an elective class was created so that our interested students could learn the techniques. These students were so motivated that they even visited the adjacent elementary school to share their newly learned strategies with their younger counterparts.

> Discipline should not be used as a punishment or means of control, but as a way to help a child solve a problem, develop inner controls, and learn better ways of expressing feelings.

In addition to featuring our prevention programs, the report went on to talk about the philosophy our school had developed, ensuring that all students would feel themselves a true part of their school. We indeed focused on the emotional and social aspects of a student's development to ensure that there was a balance with the student's academic growth. After interviewing myself as well as other staff members, the authors of the report wrote the following statement regarding our philosophy: "No child should be neglected or disregarded."

Afterthoughts and Reflections

What programs are in place for at-risk students?

_____

_____

_____

What professional development offerings are available for teachers in the area of at-risk students?

_____

_____

_____

What programs are in place to reach out to the parents of at-risk students?

_____

_____

_____

What special curricular offerings do we provide?

_____

_____

_____

What is our plan in dealing with student behavior issues?

_____

_____

_____

Which faculty members are involved in our discipline plan?

_____

_____

_____

How are we preventing or reducing out-of-school suspensions?

_____

_____

_____

6

Let's Celebrate

- Be Happy
- Spread the Word
- Best of the Best

Most people like to celebrate. When we think of celebrations, we think of happy times, and happy times are "feel-good" times. Birthdays are celebrated in families and among friends, from the time a child is one year old. In fact, births are celebrated often with balloons and greeting cards and lots of excitement. Life's milestones are also celebrated. Events such as school graduations, weddings, anniversaries, and securing new positions all are reasons for celebrations in our schools. Holidays such as Christmas and New Year's Day and Valentine's Day are often meaningful to families and friends. Celebrations bring people closer together and create connections between people. The big question here is, Do we celebrate in our schools? And if we do, do we celebrate enough?

> Celebrations bring people closer together and create connections between people.

The topic of celebration could be relegated to a paragraph or two in most books on school leadership. Actually, one reads very little about celebrations in schools, except maybe to hear about a school prom or a winning sports team. However, celebrations are a very important part of building a positive school culture with a strong foundation. One of our goals in building an exemplary school is creating a family of caring individuals. We want our teachers to care about their students, and we want our school administrators to truly care about teachers. Thomas J. Peters, management guru, once said, "Celebrate what you want to see more of." Again, it needs to be a "ripple effect," reaching out to all. Celebrations go a long way in bringing people together and in building bridges.

A thought-provoking article by Sue Shellenbarger in the November 20, 2012, issue of the *Wall Street Journal* was titled "Showing Appreciation at the Office? No, Thanks." The article notes that of all the places where people might express gratitude, the workplace is last. Although research suggests that employees who feel appreciated are more productive and loyal, says Shellenbarger, the message has not reached many in charge.

Attendance Excellence

One of our most successful celebrations at Palm Springs Middle School was the celebration of our attendance improvement. As discussed previously, our school had a long way to go in the attendance standings of the district. Our climb from number thirty-six to number one was not an easy one and would not have been possible if not for the celebrations along the way. Homerooms were really at the core of our attendance improvement efforts, so the celebrations began there. Schoolwide morning announcements celebrated the homeroom groups with perfect attendance for the day and week. Often our administrators would go into the top homerooms with doughnuts to celebrate their winning records. To carry this ritual a bit further, our videographer would often film the students enjoying their reward, and the video would be shown to the entire school on the following day. It was a fun activity that showed appreciation, built positive relationships, and promoted our attendance goal.

Celebrations for attendance did not stop at the homeroom level but continued with pizza parties before the close of the day for weekly winners. Public announcements were always an appreciated form of recognition, especially when it promoted competition and built school pride. There were six middle schools in our particular region, and it was always cause for celebration when we were number one in the region. It was rather like the excitement a school or even a community feels when its football team wins a big game. Even our cafeteria manager got into the act, baking chocolate chip cookies and passing them out to all students as they entered the cafeteria for lunch after we reached a top attendance achievement.

Of course, the rental of a giant helium balloon to be placed atop our school auditorium was truly visible proof of our attendance achievement. The balloon was quite large and could be seen from a considerable distance. It had a large "#1" banner wrapped around it and was even lit up at night. The students and teachers were quite impressed with this display, as were parents and other community members who would drive by the school. We kept the balloon for a week, but its memory lasted. After all, it is not every day that a school can celebrate in this way. Celebrations are motivating and reinforcing for all.

Scholastic Excellence

A major celebration for our students and their families was our quarterly honor roll celebration, as mentioned previously. We had a rather large auditorium, like the ones built many years ago, which held some 600 people. The auditorium was always filled with student honor roll members and their families. Families loved this event and often attended with siblings and grandparents. These were great pride-building events as well as a parental involvement activity. Our school band or chorus was always honored to be asked to perform a few numbers during the ceremony. At the conclusion of our honor roll celebrations, students and their families were invited to the cafeteria for juice and cookies and picture taking. One of our secretaries was particularly talented at using an instant camera, which put photos of families on buttons they could then wear with pride. Not only was this event a great celebration, it was also a collaborative and pride-building activity, all crucial elements of a successful school.

Celebrating students should be a central part of any school's basic core. After all, it is the mission of adults in a school to improve student achievement and to help mold successful adults. It is all about students. Remember that we are in a people business, and the success of our people is what it is all about. Having a strong middle school philosophy led us to create the "student of the month" team award. Each team of teachers (we had ten teams) would select one student each month to be recognized. The recognition could be for academic achievement, for exceptional improvement or "turnaround," or for a personal contribution made by the student to the team.

> Remember that we are in a people business, and the success of our people is what it is all about.

I'm on TV

To be on television is often a very memorable occasion for students. TV is a big part of a student's life at home, and to be on TV at school is exciting. Our closed-circuit TV morning announcements provided the perfect vehicle for celebrations, so our students of the month were invited to receive their recognition on TV. As the principal, I would call each student's name and present the student with a small trophy. Celebrations such as these are motivating and reinforcing, not only for the recipients but for others as well. Students often asked teachers what they could do to be recognized as well. As human beings, most of us do like to be recognized and appreciated for our efforts, and celebrations do just that. As Maya Angelou said, "People will forget what you said, people will forget what you did, but people will never forget how you made them feel."

As a middle school, we had various athletic and scholastic competitions with other schools. Our after-school sports teams competed with neighboring middle schools and at times went on to wider district competitions. Our Future Business Leaders of America, our Future Educators of America, and our Future Homemakers of America were active participants in district and state competitions, thanks to great teacher leadership. Band and chorus competitions were annual events, and our teacher-directors were most competitive. Our groups usually received top honors in district evaluations and would come home with a trophy or two. All of these events were celebrated with TV recognition and schoolwide admiration.

Recognition

Having a large electronic marquee in the front of our school proved to be a wonderful way to announce celebrations. Any time we had a reason to celebrate, or a cause to be proud of, it was posted on the marquee. This manner of what might be considered "advertising" was a simple and effective way to publicize the good things that were happening at our school. Again, celebrations build pride, and one of our goals was to increase pride in our school and the positive things that were happening. We wanted to make sure our parents and community members could share with us. As Lord Byron, the renowned Scottish poet, said, "To have joy, one must share it."

There was an inspiring article in the January 7, 2011, issue of *Inc.* magazine titled "10 Tips for Boosting Employee Morale" (Hames, 2011).

Inc. is a business-oriented publication featuring stories of up-and-coming companies, with an annual list of the fastest growing new companies. The number one tip in this feature article was "Recognize special events in the lives of your employees." If business leaders are encouraged to practice employee recognition, how about educators? Says the article's author, "Birthdays, weddings, births, the accomplishments of employee children—if you have a reason to celebrate, do it!"

Adults in our building were never forgotten. We managed to find ways to celebrate everyday events as well as special recognitions. A birthday was always recognized with a special birthday card placed in the teacher's mailbox on the day of the event. Our cafeteria workers were always especially appreciative to be included along with teachers. If a faculty member's birthday happened to fall on a faculty meeting day, a birthday cake was shared by all. A successful school needs to be like a happy family, sharing in the good fortunes of all members.

> As school leaders, the more we can do to foster collegiality, the better off we will be as a school family.

We celebrated the special events in one another's lives, such as weddings, graduations, births, honors and recognitions, and anything else that brought pride to our lives. Because we had faculty meetings on a twice-monthly basis, there was always an opportunity to catch up with the good things that were happening. Knowing about our fellow faculty members and caring about them goes a long way toward building and maintaining a positive school culture. We have all probably attended conferences and meetings at which the participants are basically strangers to one another. Often the leader will introduce what are called "ice breakers," which are simple and quick activities to help participants get to know a little something about one another. Immediately, there is a building of rapport and an increase in one's comfort level. As school leaders, the more we can do to foster collegiality, the better off we will be as a school family.

Best of the Year

Of course, there were the bigger events, such as the Teacher of the Year award. Most schools do have some type of recognition for a teacher or teachers who seem to go above and beyond the norm. Our teacher of the year was always selected by the entire teaching staff and was therefore special because it was a choice of one's peers. The big announcement was always made on morning TV, with follow-up on the marquee. Often a paragraph or two was written in the local newspaper, and an article would appear in our school newspaper.

We were fortunate to have two of our administrators be recognized as district winners. One of our assistant principals was chosen Administrator of the Year for Exceptional Student Education. This was a well-deserved award, as she had done much to integrate the various student exceptionalities into the total school program and indeed had built an outstanding program. As with all recognitions, this award brought great pride to the school, and pride is a builder of positive culture. Both teachers and students now had a greater connection to their school with a feeling of being winners. As Oprah Winfrey was quoted as saying, "The more you praise and celebrate your life, the more there is in life to celebrate."

My "claim to fame" was being chosen Principal of the Year for the entire school district of some 300-plus principals. This recognition took place during my third year as principal, and the teachers and students and parents all knew that I was in the running. Excitement grew when I was one of just six finalists, and there were stories and pictures in the *Miami Herald*. The announcement of the winner was made at a luncheon that was attended by hundreds of school and community leaders. Word of my selection had reached the school before I could get back, and when I drove into the parking lot it seemed as though half the school was cheering. Interviews appeared on local TV news stations, along with articles in the newspapers about our wonderful school. To say that the prestige of our school increased a notch would be an understatement. The recognition, celebration, and ensuing pride were wonderful for a school previously overlooked. You might say that this was true recognition of our successful turnaround efforts.

Neila Connors, the author of *If You Don't Feed the Teachers, They Eat the Students!* talked about celebrations in a chapter called "Meaningful Experiences Affecting Long-Term Success." To quote Connors, "Leaders who celebrate provide the vehicle to strengthen and improve morale and raise the success level of schooling. Through celebrations, achievements are recognized, people are encouraged, and experiences are shared." Let us always remember that we are in a people business and that people have emotions and feelings. Whether we are talking about our students or our teachers or our parents, everyone needs to feel "celebrated" to be truly effective.

Afterthoughts and Reflections

How do we celebrate our teachers?

_____

_____

_____

What are our student celebrations?

_____

_____

_____

What celebrations might we add?

_____

_____

_____

What message are we taking away from this chapter?

_____

_____

_____

7

Coaching Strategies at Work

- Ask, Don't Tell
- Bring on the Brilliance
- Listen and Reflect
- From Teachers to Students

There is probably nothing more important in successful endeavors than relationships. All of us are part of families. If the relationship among the members of a family is a caring and supportive one, the family members have a better chance at success in life. Most of us have been employed while attending school or after school. The success we have in those jobs often depends on the relationships formed with our colleagues and supervisors. The relationships we form in our schools can predict the level of success we will achieve as a school family.

Coaching is one very powerful strategy in building positive and successful relationships in our schools. The term "coaching" often takes on many different meanings. Our definition will be quite specific and different from what most people probably think and will be explained as we progress in this chapter. When most people think of a coach, they think of the coaches they may have had growing up, as they experimented with different sports. Everyone is familiar with little league, high school, and college sports coaches. The role of these coaches is to help players improve by instructing, by focusing on strengths and weaknesses, and by directing practices.

The popular and growing area of "life coaching" is a relatively new movement that has gained wide popularity. A life coach is someone whose purpose is to help a client live a more successful and meaningful life. People hire life coaches to help them sort through situations they may be having in their lives. The life coaching industry has broadened to include coaches with specific areas of expertise. We can now find coaches who specialize in working with single women, parents with child-raising issues, job seekers, marriage issues, and a range of other personal situations for which people may seek support. The International Coach Federation was formed in 1995 and now has over 18,000 members worldwide. Both Columbia University and Harvard University offer courses toward coaching certification. Coaching is truly big business.

Schools too have begun to use reading coaches, math coaches, and literacy coaches to help teachers improve their skills and increase their knowledge. These coaches are usually experts in their fields and are considered to be master teachers. Their services can be especially beneficial to new teachers and to teachers who are experimenting with new curricula. In actuality, these "coaches" are mentors who observe and instruct, quite different from the leadership coaching I will be outlining. Often the funds to support a coaching program such as this will come from federal grants.

Leadership Coaching

Coaching can be a new tool or strategy to be used by a school principal, as long as one realizes that it is quite different from the other forms of coaching used in schools. Leadership coaching is not mentoring, nor is it counseling. As the sixteenth-century Italian scientist and philosopher Galileo said, "You cannot teach a man anything; you can only help him find it within himself." This is a very powerful thought, and said so very long ago. Coaching strategies may well help school leaders keep this in mind. Ross Hunefeld (2009), of Noble Street Charter School in Chicago, wrote, "What my school is learning, and what current research suggests, is that teachers don't improve by listening to someone tell them how to do something newer or better in their classrooms."

> Coaching can be a new tool or strategy to be used by a school principal.

Our leadership coaching strategies are about collaborating with our staff in a way that will help them uncover their own strengths and expertise. Leadership coaching is about asking relevant questions instead of telling unwanted ideas. It is about listening in a meaningful way rather than jumping into a conversation just to be heard. It is about providing feedback so as to encourage personal reflection. Finally, it is about setting goals and taking action. David Rock and Jeffrey Schwartz (2006), in their article "A Brain-Based Approach to Coaching," suggested the acronym ARIA, for attention, reflection, insight, and action, to remind us to lead by helping others focus attention on an issue, reflect on solutions, gain new insights, and then take action.

We know people are resistant to change, yet for a turnaround leader, change is inevitable. Coaching teaches us that learning to ask important questions does indeed bring about the changes we may be looking for. "Questions hold the power to cause us to think, create answers we believe in, and motivate us to act on our ideas" (Stoltzfus, 2008).

> Coaching teaches us that learning to ask important questions does indeed bring about the changes we may be looking for.

Let's look at the following list to get an idea of the power of questions in promoting thinking and subsequent change:

- What worked well for you this week?
- What problems did you encounter?
- What can you do differently?
- What might you focus on?
- How do you feel about that?
- What are your challenges now?
- What is your game plan?
- If your classroom could look the way you would like it to look, what would that be?
- What do you need to resolve this challenge?

These questions are only a few examples of coaching conversation starters. It is obvious that questions such as these, and there are many others we could use, are true thought provokers. A coaching relationship is one in which the pair becomes thinking partners. I am sure we have all had situations in which others come to us completely frustrated with what is happening in their lives. A teacher may be distraught over a particular class that is not responding the way the teacher would like. I can remember, as a first-year teacher, one of my five classes that was a particular challenge to me. The counselor offered to come to that class and talk with the students. I don't recall the outcome, but I now know that a good question to get my thinking going would have been more helpful. It is usually the case that when someone is frustrated and upset, his or her rational thinking seems to shut off. A thought-provoking question usually turns things around.

David Rock (2006), in *Quiet Leadership*, wrote, "If you want to improve performance, the most effective way to do this is to improve thinking." This is a most powerful statement for school leaders, although it is a simple reflection. What is it that school leaders are about? Aren't we about improving performance? Our goal, hopefully, is to improve the performance of our teachers so that they may improve the achievement of their students. Because coaching strategies revolve around meaningful questions that lead to improved thinking, we indeed have a powerful professional development tool in coaching. Again, David Rock, who is a neuroscientist and developer of the management coaching program at New York University, wrote in *Quiet Leadership*, "When people solve a problem themselves, the brain releases a rush of neurotransmitters like adrenaline. This phenomenon provides a scientific basis for some of the practices of leadership coaching."

> We indeed have a powerful professional development tool in coaching.

The *New York Times*, in a March 13, 2011, article, reported on employee satisfaction at Google's headquarters in California. What they found was that Google employees valued managers "who helped people puzzle through problems by asking questions, not dictating answers, and who took an interest in employees' lives and careers" (Bryant, 2011). Again, this reinforces what leadership coaching is about and what successful school leadership needs to be. Our goal is to foster collaboration and build a positive culture.

Let us use as one example the relationship between the principal and the assistant principals. Every school is different, but they do have many common areas, and one such area might be what is often called the "staff meeting." Some schools follow the practice of meeting, as the leadership team, on a weekly or biweekly basis. Some principals meet with their immediate staff on an as-needed basis. Whatever the meeting schedule might be, these times are perfect opportunities for the coaching strategy of meaningful questions to be implemented.

One scenario might revolve around the topic of implementing a new student schedule, such as a block schedule, with questions such as these:

- How do you think the faculty will react to this new and different idea?
- How about the students and parents?

- Does anyone have knowledge of the pros and cons of a plan like this?
- How might we go about presenting this to the faculty?
- Who should do the presentation?
- Can you come up with any supportive material?
- How do you personally feel about the idea?
- What do you think the outcome might be?
- Who might be our biggest supporters?
- Who might present a negative reaction?

This is just a sampling of questions that would lead to deeper thinking. The goal of significant questioning is to allow time for that thinking, which is often missed in many meetings in which just information is doled out. Additionally, questioning allows necessary buy-in from those involved. We all want to be asked what we think, as opposed to being told what to think. Of course, we are fostering a collaborative culture, so we want to work cooperatively Leadership is not an "I'll do it all because I'm the principal" philosophy. The objective is to share intelligence and to be the bandleader, and coaching questions can lead to that objective.

> We all want to be asked what we think, as opposed to being told what to think.

Effective Teachers

One of our goals in becoming exemplary school leaders is to have a staff of truly effective teachers. Hopefully, we do our best in selecting new teachers when we have the opportunity. Often, we inherit teachers who may not be performing as we might like. Having meaningful conversations about classroom performance with teachers is an important part of a principal's job, as well as an assistant principal's. These necessary administrator-teacher conferences are perfect opportunities to implement the use of coaching strategies. Again, the objective is to help teachers realize what the problem areas might be and to come up with solutions they may be comfortable with.

I can recall a time, when I was an assistant principal, when we had a teacher just returning from maternity leave who was having an extremely difficult time with classroom management. Parents were complaining, and students were truly out of control. The principal and I called the teacher in for a conference. This was many years ago, and coaching questions were unheard of, but the principal conducted the conference with the use of thoughtful and compassionate questions. Knowing that our teacher was a new mother and had two other children at home and in school, the principal asked her if things were difficult at home. He asked if she had enough time to plan her lessons and whether there was anything at school we could do to help her. I remember that the teacher released a lot of emotion during the conference, which was probably something she sorely needed to do. She notified us the next day that she and her husband had agreed that she would extend her leave for the rest of the year.

Teacher evaluation has always been a major task for school administrators. We hear much about how to evaluate teachers and how often to do so and, of course, what the basis of the evaluation should be. Evaluations continue to evolve, not only for teachers but for administrators as well. School site evaluations often vary by district and are certainly different state by state. Whatever the instrument of evaluation may be, it is followed by a conference between the administrator and the teacher. Unfortunately, many of these conferences become one-way sessions, with the administrator doing all or most of the talking and the teacher trying to absorb all that went well or did not go so well.

Using coaching questions during an evaluation or observation conference can turn the time into a two-way experience, with the teacher coming away with new insights into his or her teaching practices:

- What did you feel went particularly well during today's lesson?
- Which parts of the lesson caused concern for you?
- Did you feel all students were on task?
- What strategies do you use in redirecting off-task students?
- Was there anything you feel could have been done better?
- Was there anything you needed to improve the lesson?
- How might you do the lesson differently next time?

These questions are only a few of what might be typically used in a follow-up conference. Administrators will want to interject their own observations and feelings about what they observed, and this will fit right in by providing feedback.

Feedback

In leadership coaching, feedback is always an important part of any coaching conference and comes in the form of reflection. When one practices thoughtful listening and actually absorbs what is being said, it is easy to provide feedback. In the first sample question above, about what went well, the teacher might say, "I was pleased to see that all students worked well in their group activity." The administrator might provide the needed feedback by saying, "Yes, I was particularly impressed with that part of your lesson and could see that your students are comfortable working collaboratively. Collaboration is indeed one of our goals." This type of coaching exchange helps the teacher reinforce what was positive in the observation and allows the administrator to provide input.

As a second example, looking at the question above about students on task, the teacher might reply by saying that he or she noticed two students apparently distracted when moving from group work to a computer assignment. The administrator might respond with reflective feedback along the lines of "What strategies do you usually use to redirect off-task behavior? Did you feel that intervention was needed in this particular case?" Again, this type of verbal exchange provides the teacher with an opportunity to think about and reflect upon his or her practice of dealing with off-task students and allows the administrator an opportunity to offer suggestions. "Do you feel that the topic of redirecting students might be appropriate for a professional learning community session?" might be a perfect response on the part of the administrator.

Ken Blanchard is probably one of the most widely read authors on the subject of management. His *One Minute Manager*, coauthored with Spencer Johnson, has sold over 13 million copies and has been translated into dozens of languages (Blanchard & Johnson, 1982). In this powerful book, Blanchard wrote, "I believe providing feedback is the most cost effective strategy for improving performance and instilling satisfaction." It is interesting to note that in this simple sentence, we see two very important goals for us as school leaders: improving performance and instilling satisfaction. Providing feedback is an important element in leadership coaching and can indeed be a powerful tool.

Opportunities for providing feedback are abundant throughout the school day, not only at conference time. We talked much about being a visible leader and about doing classroom walk-throughs on a regular basis. To refer back to Blanchard's comment on instilling satisfaction, our walk-throughs are perfect vehicles for feedback on what was observed: "Your science lesson on DNA today could not have been better"

> Providing time to listen to the teacher, without interruption, and with patience, is a wonderful gift and an especially crucial part of a coaching relationship.

or "You certainly are talented at getting even the most reluctant student to participate." These comments obviously go a long way in bringing about teacher satisfaction while reinforcing good teaching.

Thinking time is important in all leadership coaching conversations and is especially important in a conference after a teacher's classroom observation. Our purpose in such a conference is not only to review the teacher's performance but to provide the teacher with an opportunity to think about how the lesson actually played out. This is where good listening skills are especially important. Often in the busy schedule of a school administrator, the mode of operation is one of rushing from one activity to another, without the opportunity to catch one's breath. Providing time to listen to the teacher, without interruption, and with patience, is a wonderful gift and an especially crucial part of a coaching relationship. I read a message in a fortune cookie not long ago that said "Nature gave us one tongue and two ears so we could hear twice as much as we speak." Most apropos!

Student Relationships

We can see that leadership coaching strategies can be a wonderful tool, leading to the creation of an exemplary school. Leadership coaching builds collaboration among the administrative staff and provides excellent support for teachers while fostering positive relationships. Learning and practicing the coaching skills of questioning and listening and providing feedback can also be a powerful tool in the success of professional learning communities. Additionally, there is another possible area in which coaching strategies can come into play, and that is in the relationships between teachers and students. A coaching relationship of asking and listening is quite different from the teacher-student model of telling and directing.

A positive learning environment needs to be a two-way street, today more than ever. Young people are living in an interactive world, often from the time they begin to walk, and probably before they learn to talk. They want to be involved and participatory as well. I often reminded my faculty of the familiar saying about the "sage on the stage" and the "guide on the side." A teacher needs to be that guide and observer and facilitator. Teachers need to ask those questions that stimulate thinking in students, and that is where our coaching strategies can be most important.

Coaching with students can follow the same pattern as coaching with adults. Are we asking thought-provoking questions of our students, as opposed to simple questions with yes-or-no answers?

- What influenced you to select this particular book?
- What is your plan for completing your report?
- How will you divide the group responsibilities?
- Where will you find the material for your project?
- Who might be able to help you with this?
- What might have caused that conflict, and how will you solve it?
- What can you do so that that does not become an issue again?
- What is preventing you from completing your home assignments?
- What system do you use to plan out your work?
- How would you like to present your next book study?
- What deficits do you feel you have regarding your math work?
- How can I help you?
- What would you need to do if you wanted to improve your grade?

These are just a few of the possible interactions between a teacher and a student. The questioning will certainly vary depending on the age and grade level of the student. However, all questions should lead to thoughtful introspection on the part of the student. We want our students to think and to come up with their own solutions. As good listeners, with one tongue and two ears, we want to give our students ample time to think through their answers. Often, a bit of silence while thinking is a good thing. Silence can be uncomfortable in a conversation but can show a student that you are truly listening.

> We want our students to think and to come up with their own solutions.

Goal Setting

Thinking about goals is a very important part of the practice of coaching, and all coaching includes the setting of goals. Good questioning on the part of a teacher, which can lead students to be thoughtful, can also help them think about goals. Tony Robbins, one of the most recognizable motivational speakers and authors, said, "Setting goals is the first step in turning the invisible into the visible." Do we as teachers ever talk with students about setting goals for themselves?

- What grade do you expect to receive in this class, and how will you go about achieving that?
- How will you go about completing your science project?
- How do you know that you are working toward your goal of reading two novels per month?
- Which subject will turn out to be your best grade on your final report card, and how will you work to achieve that?
- Where are you, so far, in completing your social studies project?

These are just a very few examples of thought-provoking goal questions. They are an important part of coaching strategies and can serve as a tool to help students remain focused. If students are working in groups, goal setting can be a wonderful topic for a group discussion. Students like to share their progress as well as their setbacks. Of course, writing down their goals and referring to them periodically is an important part of this very valuable process.

We hear much conversation in the national media about students needing to be college or career ready when they graduate. Of course, we also hear as much conversation about students not graduating at all. Sharpstown High School in Houston, Texas, has what is called a graduation coach. Other schools may have the same or similar positions, whose purpose is to help students graduate. Coaching questions and goal setting are again valuable tools. Some schools, the KIPP charter schools being one example, post college banners around the school buildings, and all teachers prominently display their own alma maters. Students are asked to begin thinking about a future when they too will be attending college.

Developing a coaching relationship of thoughtful questions, real listening, and goal awareness can be a motivating factor for students. As Ralph Waldo Emerson said, "Our chief want is someone who will inspire us to be what we know we could be." Are we, as teachers, taking the time to actually inspire our students?

Coaching for Me

As mentioned previously, leadership coaching provides a one-on-one "thinking partner." Let's "think" for a moment about the positive effect a coaching relationship might have for a busy school administrator. First of all, having someone to listen to us, especially in the busy world we live in today, is truly a powerful opportunity. When we are listened to, we are given the opportunity to hear our thoughts and to clarify our thinking. Having someone ask significant questions of us provides an opportunity to clarify and solidify our ideas. Thoughts and ideas often take on different meanings when said aloud.

We have covered the concept of goal setting for teachers and students. Setting goals is certainly a major part of any school leader's responsibilities. As the famous Yankee baseball player Yogi Berra said, "If you don't know where you are going, you'll end up someplace else." Goals must be in place to guide the direction of a school, following its mission and vision. Goals must be in place to provide direction for the principal, and in most cases, the principal's evaluation is based on the accomplishment of those goals. Having a coaching relationship, with perhaps a colleague, is a powerful way to review one's progress toward goal accomplishment. The Round Rock Independent School District, in central Texas, employs a full-time leadership coach to support administrators within the district.

Coaching is an excellent vehicle for professional development activities, whether we are talking about teachers or administrators. Teachers are often involved in professional learning communities and can use the coaching strategies of listening and reflecting and providing feedback in their work. Because coaching is ongoing, it often provides much-needed support and opportunities for growth. Administrators can be involved in similar professional development through their own collegial relationships.

Afterthoughts and Reflections

What different coaching models are being used in our school?

_____

_____

_____

In what ways am I using leadership coaching strategies?

_____

_____

_____

In what ways do I provide meaningful feedback?

_____

_____

_____

How can we improve teacher-student relationships?

_____

_____

_____

What opportunities are there for me to focus on the goals of others?

_____

_____

_____

Which teachers motivated me, as a student, and how did they do so?

_____

_____

_____

How might I look at forming a meaningful coaching relationship?

_____

_____

_____

Check out:

http://www.coachfederation.org

http://www.tc.columbia.edu/coachingcertification

http://www.gse.harvard.edu/news-impact/2011/11/executive-coaching-refines-leadership-skills

http://www.scps.nyu.edu/academics/departments/leadership/academic-offerings/graduate/gc-in-organizational-and-executive-coaching.html

8

Parents Welcome

- Team Philosophy
- Multiple Approaches
- Changing Environment
- Keeping Up Appearances

Parental involvement has long been a major topic for all school leaders. Building partnerships with parents is often a top item on any school improvement plan. Being a Title I school, and therefore receiving supplemental federal funds, Palm Springs Middle School was required to include the position of parent liaison specialist. The responsibility of this person was to develop programs of interest for parents and then to publicize the events. Often it took actual home visits to encourage parents to attend school events. It is imperative that a school have a person on staff whose responsibility it is to be a liaison between the school and home.

In a recent issue of *Responsive Classroom Newsletter*, Ed Barnwell (2013), a Vermont principal, suggested the following strategies for parental outreach: be visible when parents are coming and going, make an effort to connect with parents you don't know, show interest in families' interests, make good-news phone calls, greet new families personally, and invite families for coffee or lunch. This certainly reflects a strong emphasis on building relationships.

Our middle school team philosophy, with a schedule of morning parent meetings, proved to be a major vehicle for parental involvement.

During these meetings, usually functioning three mornings a week, as many as eight team-leader classrooms would be conducting conferences with one or two families each. It brought me great pleasure to walk through our halls before the start of the students' day and to look into these rooms of active parental involvement.

Being a School-Based Management/Shared Decision Making school required us to have monthly meetings to discuss the state of the school. These meetings were announced publicly through the district and were open to all. There were requirements as to who was to be part of these meetings. In addition to the principal, there were teachers elected by their colleagues and students elected by their peers. Parents were also included and were required to be elected by the parent community. This was an excellent way for parents to actually be part of the decision-making process for the school while learning firsthand about the school budget, curriculum, and other matters. Decisions were usually made by vote, and parents were included in the voting process.

Most schools, if not all schools, hold some form of open house at the start of each school year. Usually these events are the most heavily attended events of the school year and provide an opportunity to "showcase" the school. Our procedure was to begin the evening with a closed-circuit TV presentation piped into each homeroom class. Parents were able to hear brief remarks from the principal and to be introduced to the other administrators as well as to the counselors. From this opening session, parents were invited to follow their children's schedule by moving from class to class in ten-minute increments. This time provided an opportunity for teachers to briefly explain what the school year might look like for students in each particular class. Parents always left with a very positive feeling about their children's school.

As discussed in a previous chapter, our parent report card pickup proved to be a very successful parental involvement activity. Additionally, the success of our performing arts programs was also instrumental in bringing parents to the school at performance time. Our PTA conducted quarterly meetings, often with special speakers of interest to parents, and also put on the customary spaghetti and holiday dinners. Our evening counseling sessions for parents, along with parent education programs such as test preparation and computer skills, helped round out our efforts at parental involvement.

Paradigm Shift

Today we are seeing the need for a very different focus on parents. The world of parental choice has grown rapidly in a way never seen before. Charter schools have become a true option for parents in almost every community. Parents now want to know which schools might have the best programs for their children. States are grading schools so that everyone can know which are the "A" schools and which are the "F" schools. The "parent trigger" law, approved for implementation in some states, allows parents to "take over" their neighborhood schools if they are failing. In many states, parents are provided vouchers that allow them to transfer their children from failing schools to successful schools, maybe even to private schools.

How does all this change involving parents' rights have an effect on parental involvement and the role of the principal? Parents now have to be "won over" through the creation of an exemplary school and state-of-the-art marketing by the principal. I was most surprised, during a recent visit to my former school, when the current principal explained to me that marketing the school was now a top priority. The school enrollment had gone from the previous 1,800 down to 900 and now back up to 1,200. The reason for the drop in enrollment was not any boundary changes or changes in the community but the opening of charter schools and the creation of a science magnet in a nearby public school.

> Parents now have to be "won over" through the creation of an exemplary school and state-of-the-art marketing by the principal.

During my tenure as principal, all students living within our district-established boundaries were required to attend their neighborhood schools. We were proud of our accomplishments in turning around a deficient school and indeed had developed a positive reputation in the community, to the extent that students from neighboring communities were interested in transferring to our school. However, unlike today, there was no actual competition factor. Except for private schools, with their tuition expense for parents, students and parents had no choice to speak of. Parents knew that where they lived was the primary factor determining which schools their children would attend. Today, that has all changed or is in the process of changing rapidly. I believe we are witnessing a true paradigm shift in the way public education is to be delivered to students and their families.

The *Wall Street Journal*, in its October 12, 2012, issue, ran a story titled "Uptown Schools Uproar," in which it outlined plans to allow parents to choose any one of the twenty-four elementary schools in New York City's District 6, in upper Manhattan, regardless of where they lived (Fleisher & Fox, 2012). If a particular school had reached capacity, it would hold a lottery similar to the process being carried out by successful charter schools. If I were a principal of one of these twenty-four schools, I would do all I could to create a school all families would seek to attend. Competition, such as that found in the business world, may well be what all school leaders must consider. Just as failing businesses are forced to close, failing schools will also be closed, and many throughout the country are facing this possibility.

Marketing

The big question for school leaders, most certainly, has to be "How do I create a school that will be appealing to parents, and how will I market it?" Obviously, all schools aim to have the very best teachers and the most relevant curricula to meet the needs of all students. However, these elements are often not readily visible to parents. What is visible at first is the appearance of the school and how a visitor is made to feel upon entering. When I became principal, my school had no fencing, no landscaping, and no recent painting. It was not at all attractive, so beautification became a top priority.

School leaders need to make sure that when parents and community members enter their school, they get a positive feeling right away.

- Is the entrance area clean and attractive?
- Do visitors see displays of student work, awards, and trophies?
- Is there a clean and comfortable seating area for visitors?
- Is the office staff eager to greet visitors with a welcoming smile?
- Are visitors' needs handled expeditiously?
- Does the office area appear businesslike?

I can recall that one of the first purchases made upon my arrival was a trophy case to display trophies in our main office. Parents and visitors always enjoy seeing various trophies and what they represent. Trophies, medals, ribbons, plaques, and other awards plainly say "We are winners," and people do want to be associated with winners.

How does the rest of the building look? Are the hallways generally clean and the walls free of writing? I recall that cleaning walls and keeping them clean was an early task I assigned to our custodial crew. The faculty had become accustomed to walls often scribbled with markers and for the most part did not give this a second thought. There is no doubt that a clean building sends a positive message to all and says, "We care." The purchase of hallway bulletin boards was a big help in keeping the walls attractive. All team leaders were assigned boards, usually right outside their classrooms, where they could post items relevant to their teams' activities.

How do the classrooms appear to visitors? Again, we are looking at an age of school competition when parents may want to see a typical class in action. I can recall my pride when visitors would come to our school and I could give them a tour, knowing that they would be impressed. Visitors need to see clean classrooms with evidence of student work displayed throughout. Are books and computers readily available for students' use, and are students working in an orderly fashion? Is the teacher up and about and working with students?

> First impressions are often lasting impressions.

We hear from time to time the expression "perception is reality." If parents feel that what is happening in your school is a positive thing, that is the belief they will come away with, and that is the message they may impart to others. First impressions are often lasting impressions; therefore, what a parent, community member, or any visitor for that matter sees upon entering your school is crucial.

Communication

When I became a principal in the 1990s, our main form of communication with parents was through letters of information sent home with students. We all knew that the information often did not make it home. Today, we have a world of communication options, and it is crucial that we use these means. Parental involvement through parental communication will go a long way in promoting our schools and in keeping our parents well informed.

Most parents today have e-mail accounts and use them at work and with their friends and families. Schools need to use this means of communication on a regular basis, whether it comes from the principal or from the teacher or from both. Parents love to hear from the school principal with updates on school happenings as well as events to come and, of course, celebratory happenings. Teachers need to communicate on a regular basis regarding curriculum, home assignments, tests, and upcoming events. I know of one school in particular whose teachers send a weekly e-mail describing what was studied during the week and posting photos of the students in action. One teacher even posts videos of the students at work. These are wonderful positive forms of parental involvement. Many schools are using software programs that allow parents and students to regularly check grades as well as daily attendance.

Schools now have their own websites, which are viewable by anyone and can be excellent marketing tools as well as resources for parents. Referring back to my former school, its website has anything and everything a parent or interested individual would want to know (http://palmspringsmiddle.dadeschools.net). One of the features of the website is a video made by the students that showcases the school and its offerings. Truly a wonderful marketing tool! Obviously this is just one example. Most schools have similar excellent websites, which are becoming more sophisticated all the time.

There is another important area of parental communication, and that is what we might refer to as the "other side of the coin." Parents want to be able to reach out to their children's teachers, counselors, assistant principals, and even principals. KIPP, one of the most successful charter school networks, provides cell phones for its teachers so that parents and students can reach them with questions and concerns after school hours. A successful school will make sure that all communications from parents and others are answered in a timely fashion. Parents will often "spread the word" about positive forms of school communication, and this too is a part of parental involvement.

> Parents want to be able to reach out to their children's teachers, counselors, assistant principals, and even principals.

The school website often has links to faculty members, who may have their own websites and always have their own e-mail addresses. This provides another opportunity for parent-teacher interaction. Accessibility of teachers, counselors, and administrators is most important in today's world of instant communication. Social media of the Facebook and Twitter variety extend and broaden communication. Many schools have their own Facebook pages and Twitter accounts, which open further avenues of communication and of course marketing as well.

Afterthoughts and Reflections

What activities does our school have for parents?

_____

_____

_____

_____

_____

Whose responsibility is it to oversee parental involvement?

_____

_____

_____

What new activities might we consider to increase parental involvement?

_____

_____

_____

How do we market our school?

_____

_____

_____

What additions might we make to our school website?

_____

_____

_____

What things can we do to improve the attractiveness of our school?

_____

_____

_____

9

Where We Are Now

- Building on a Strong Foundation
- Charters Bring Competition
- Technology Expanded

It was my great pleasure to be invited to visit my former school by its current principal some nine years after my departure. As my wife and I drove up to the campus, we could immediately see that the school was being maintained in outstanding fashion. What a far cry from our first visit, when I had just been appointed principal, and my wife and I found a torn-up lawn with an abandoned car as its centerpiece. The front of the building now stood tall and proud, with a new façade and an expanded parking lot and beautiful landscaping. Obviously, this was a school exhibiting pride in its home.

It was the principal's idea to keep my visit a surprise, so my wife and I were sequestered in an office while the principal began a faculty meeting. At the appointed time, we were ushered into the meeting by the secretary. It was most rewarding to be received with a standing ovation and to be able to reminisce with the faculty about where we were when we began our turnaround. Approximately half of the current faculty were part of our transformation, and the newer half had certainly heard about it.

Sustainability

A big part of a school turnaround effort is whether it can be sustainable. Were the programs significant enough to endure? Did the faculty really buy in to the newfound culture? Did student achievement continue to increase? Was the school still viewed as a desirable environment for all students? Was the foundation strong enough to still be standing and to allow additional growth? Or was this a story of "this too shall pass"? I strongly believe that our turnaround efforts, which focused on a strong foundation of collaboration and positive relationships, allowed the initiatives to flourish and to expand. The turnaround story was not one of top-down directives but one of true team building and respect for the ideas of all stakeholders.

> A big part of a school turnaround effort is whether it can be sustainable.

The state of Florida began issuing letter grades to schools as part of its accountability initiative a few years before my departure. Although we started out with a C, we did rise to a B, while many of the district's middle schools remained at the C level or could not progress from a D. The grades were based on test scores, mostly in the areas of math and language arts and writing, with science gradually being added. Palm Springs Middle School has since been able to reach the A level and is indeed recognized for its academic accomplishments in meeting the needs of its varied demographics.

More time on task is often highlighted as an important ingredient in increasing student achievement. The unique block schedule of rotating classes, which was one of our major turnaround initiatives, is still functioning beautifully. Teachers enjoy meeting classes at different times of the day, and students are profiting from a ninety-minute block of time on task.

School uniforms are still in place, with full support from both parents and students. As I toured the school, it was gratifying to see what seemed to be 100 percent adherence to the uniform policy. An addition to the original uniform policy is that students' shirts are now color coded to their grade levels. Because many of the school areas are grade specific, this helps in identifying students who may not be where they belong.

Miami-Dade County Public Schools conducts a school climate survey on a yearly basis. The survey is completed by parents, students, and staff and provides an awareness of the feelings these stakeholders may have about a school. Additionally, each school is compared with all other schools in the district within its grade level. The most recent survey highlighted several factors indicating that Palm Springs parents were indeed pleased with where the school is:

	Palm Springs Middle School	Districtwide
Cleanliness of school	96%	80%
Satisfaction with programs	89%	83%
Teachers interested in students' futures	92%	81%
The principal runs the school well	92%	84%
Counselors help students	89%	76%
Staff treat parents with respect	95%	88%
Students are getting a good education	95%	89%

Students appreciate having their voices heard and enjoy completing their own opinion surveys. The recent climate survey indicated an overall positive reaction to school life:

	Palm Springs Middle School	Districtwide
Teachers are friendly	58%	62%
Teachers are interested in me	58%	63%
The principal does a good job	54%	67%
Assistant principals are available	58%	58%
Counselors help me	68%	56%

Staff members are of course a most important part of any climate survey, and their overall satisfaction at work is an important indicator of the state of the school:

	Palm Springs Middle School	Districtwide
Teamwork is evident	78%	81%
My ideas are listened to	70%	75%
The principal is effective	94%	83%
The principal supports teachers	84%	82%
The principal represents the school positively	92%	88%
The principal treats teachers with respect	84%	89%

It is certainly encouraging to realize that the stakeholders of Palm Springs Middle School do view the school in a positive light. Most recently, the school system was awarded the coveted Broad Prize for Urban Education. Only one school system in the nation is awarded this distinction each year, and it is based on increased student achievement and reducing the achievement gap. What makes this award even more special is that Palm Springs Middle School was one of the schools visited by the Broad selection committee. This was indeed an honor for the school and its staff, students, and parents.

Competition Has Arrived

> The answer came to me in two words: charter schools.

It was a bit of an eye-opener for me when I asked about the current enrollment and was told that the numbers had decreased by half since the days of 1,800 students. I knew that the community had been stable, and I had not heard of any new school construction that may have been responsible for siphoning students from the school. The answer came to me in two words: charter schools.

Indeed, the charter school movement had begun in the area prior to my departure, but the few charter schools that were in place basically served as alternative schools for students not meeting with success in their home schools. Now a different picture was being painted, in that the number of charter schools had increased greatly, and they were now offering programs of interest to all student populations. The charter schools were actively recruiting students from traditional public schools and were eager to announce their record of A grades in the state accountability ratings. Additionally, one of the neighboring middle schools had recently been converted to a magnet school specializing in science and technology. This school too was heavily recruiting students throughout the area. The days of neighborhood schools with strict attendance boundaries appear to have ended. School choice has arrived.

A new dimension has apparently been added to the role of public school principal: that of recruiter. It is no longer a viable option for a school to sit back and wait for students who live within its attendance boundaries to knock on the door. The world of school choice has made it necessary for today's principals to actively step outside the school walls and go where prospective students might be. The current principal of my former school informed me that he regularly visits elementary schools where prospective future students are to be found. Fortunately, the school has built upon the positive reputation created during our turnaround efforts. Now the task is to show students and their parents what the school has to offer.

School choice has arrived.

A centerpiece of the school's recruitment efforts is a well-made video featuring student testimonials. My wife and I enjoyed viewing the video in the principal's office during our visit and were impressed with the excellent student presentations. Not only was the delivery of high quality, but the school areas highlighted were impressive. The video appeared to do its job of featuring bright students who showed enthusiasm for their school. The students focused on the various academic classes as well as the special areas and of course the electives, such as band and chorus. Technology was strongly emphasized, and the video showed its integration in all class areas. Such programs as Scholastic FASTT Math and Fraction Nation, Reading Plus, Gizmos, and TeenBiz are widely used to assist in student achievement. Several parent testimonials closed out this very important recruitment tool.

Back in our early school turnaround days, technology was beginning to have its voice heard. Our technology initiatives included not only bringing computers into the school but also creating a website and using e-mail to communicate with our parents. Today's typical school website has grown dramatically and includes everything prospective parents and students might want to know. The Palm Springs website serves as an excellent recruitment tool, complete with a link to the student video. Its featured motto is "People reaching incredible dreams through education": certainly a beautiful thought to focus on.

Resources

Palm Springs Middle School: http://palmspringsmiddle.dadeschools.net

School climate surveys: http://drs.dadeschools.net/SchoolClimateSurvey/SCS.asp

Broad Prize for Urban Education: http://broadprize.org

FASTT Math: http://teacher.scholastic.com/fraction-fluency/fraction-nation/

Fraction Nation: http://teacher.scholastic.com/fraction-fluency/fraction-nation/

TeenBiz: http://www.teenbiz3000.com

Reading Plus: http://www.readingplus.com

Gizmos: http://www.explorelearning.com

References

Barnwell, E. (2013, Winter). Parent outreach for busy leaders. *Responsive Classroom Newsletter*, pp. 14–15.

Ben-Shahar, T. (2007). *Happier: Learn the secrets to daily joy and lasting fulfillment.* New York: McGraw-Hill.

Blanchard, K., & Johnson, S. (1982). *The one minute manager.* New York: William Morrow.

Bryant, A. (2009, July 11). At Yum Brands, rewards for good work. *New York Times.* Retrieved from http://www.nytimes.com/2009/07/12/business/12corner.html?pagewanted=all&_r=0

Bryant, A. (2010, November 20). Can you handle the 100-day to-do list? Retrieved from www.nytimes.com/2010/11/21/business/21corner.html?pagewanted=all&_r=0

Bryant, A. (2011, March 13). Google's quest to build a better boss. *The New York Times.* Retrieved from http://www.nytimes.com/2011/03/13/business/13hire.html?pagewanted=all&_r=0

Buckingham, M., & Clifton, D. O. (2001). *Now, discover your strengths.* New York: Free Press.

The Civil Rights Project, Harvard University. (2000, June). *Opportunities suspended: The devastating consequences of zero tolerance and school discipline.* Retrieved from http://civilrightsproject.ucla.edu/research/k-12-education/school-discipline/opportunities-suspended-the-devastating-consequences-of-zero-tolerance-and-school-discipline-policies/crp-opportunities-suspended-zero-tolerance-2000.pdf

Clark, K. (2010, January). Education Secretary Arne Duncan says merit pay should be tied to student growth. *US News & World Report, 147,* 31.

Comer, J. P., & Poussaint, A. F. (1992). *Raising black children: Two leading psychiatrists confront the educational, social and emotional problems facing black children.* New York: Plume.

Connors, N. A. (2000). *If you don't feed the teachers they eat the students! Guide to success for administrators and teachers.* Nashville, TN: Incentive.

Council of State Governments Justice Center. (2011). *The School Discipline Consensus Project.* Retrieved from http://www.justicecenter.csg.org/resources/juveniles

DuFour, R. (2004). What is a professional learning community? *Educational Leadership, 61*(8), 6–11.

Fleisher, L., & Fox, A. (2012, October 12). Uptown schools uproar: Council weighs end to zones, unnerving parents who want neighborhood schools. *The Wall Street Journal*. Retrieved from http://online.wsj.com/article/SB10000872396390044329490457805300428581266 8.html

Frase, L., & Hertzel, R. (2003). *School management by wandering around*. Lancaster, PA: Technomic.

Gimenez, S. L. (2012). Leading the wagon train. *School Administrator, 69*(7), 22–25.

Goldberg, M. (2001). *Lessons from exceptional school leaders*. Alexandria, VA: ASCD.

Gruenert, S. (2008, March/April). School culture, school climate: They are not the same thing. *Principal*, pp. 56–59.

Hames, J. M. (2011, January 7). 10 tips for boosting employee morale. *Inc*. Retrieved from http://www.inc.com/guides/2011/01/10-tips-for-boosting-employee-morale.html

Hopkins, G. (2008, February 8). Principals identify top ten leadership traits. *Education World*. Retrieved from http://www.educationworld.com/a_admin/admin/admin190.shtml

Hord, S. M. (1997–1998). Professional learning communities: What are they and why are they important? *Issues . . . About Change, 6*(1). Retrieved from http://www.sedl.org/change/issues/issues61.html

Hsieh, T. (2010). *Delivering happiness: A path to profits, passion, and purpose*. New York: Business Plus.

Hunefeld, R. (2009). When teachers are the experts: How schools can improve professional development. *Education Week, 29*(10), 24–25.

Koughan, F. (Writer & Producer), & Vargas, K. (Producer). (2012). *Dropout nation*. Frontline. United States: WGBH Educational Foundation.

Marshall, K. (2008). The big rocks: Priority management for principals. *Principal Leadership, 8*(7), 16–22.

Meltzer, B. (2012, September 30). World's greatest teacher. *Parade*. Retrieved from http://www.parade.com/news/views/guest/120930-brad-meltzer-worlds-greatest-teacher.html

National Association of Elementary School Principals & National Association of Secondary School Principals. (2012, September 13). *Rethinking principal evaluation: A new paradigm informed by research and practice*. Retrieved from http://www.naesp.org/sites/default/files/PrincipalEvaluation Report.pdf

Peters, T., & Waterman, R. H., Jr. (2004). *In search of excellence: Lessons from America's best-run companies*. New York: HarperBusiness.

Reiss, K. (2012). *Be a changemaster: 12 coaching strategies for leading professional and personal change*. Thousand Oaks, CA: Corwin.

Rock, D. (2006). *Quiet leadership: Six steps to transforming performance at work*. New York: HarperCollins.

Rock, D., & Schwartz, J. M. (2006). A brain-based approach to coaching. *International Journal of Coaching in Organizations, 4*(2), 57–68.

Ruder, R. (2006). Approachability & visibility. *Principal Leadership, 7*(3), 39–41.

Shellenbarger, S. (2012, November 20). Showing appreciation at the office? No, thanks. *The Wall Street Journal*. Retrieved from http://www.online.wsj.com/article/SB10001424127887324352004578131002460783008.html

Sirotnik, K. A., & Clark, R. W. (1988). School-centered decision making and renewal. *Phi Delta Kappan, 69*(9), 660–664.

Smith, L. (2008). *Schools that change: Evidence-based improvement and effective change leadership.* Thousand Oaks, CA: Corwin.

Stoltzfus, T. (2008). *Coaching questions: A coach's guide to powerful asking skills.* Virginia Beach, VA: Author.

Teacher Leaders Network. (2008, June 12). Advice to a new principal. *Teacher.* Retrieved from http://www.edweek.org/tm/articles/2008/06/12/37tln_norton.h19.html

Weintraub, R. J. (2012). 15 lessons on leadership. *Phi Delta Kappan, 93*(7), 80.

Welch, J., & Welch, S. (2007, September 14). Keeping your people pumped. *BloombergBusinessweek.* Retrieved from http://www.businessweek.com/stories/2007-09-14/keeping-your-people-pumpedbusinessweek-business-news-stock-market-and-financial-advice

Whitaker, W. O. (Producer), & Atkinson, K. J. (Director). (1974). *Cipher in the snow* [Motion picture]. United States: Brigham Young University.

Index